Absolutely Write

(Revised Edition)

A foundation in academic writing for
natural scientists and engineers

A foundation in academic writing for
natural scientists and engineers

ABSOLUTELY WRITE

University College
Sungkyunkwan University

REVISED
EDITION

Sungkyunkwan University Press

Contents

The Writing Process

Styles of Writing

Building Blocks

Research Skills

The Writing Process

This section helps students develop and master three basic structures for scientific writing: sentences, paragraphs, and experiment reports. The first part covers different kinds of sentence structure so learners can use a variety of sentence types in their writing. The next part explores paragraphs by explaining how to brainstorm, develop parts of the paragraph, and maintain consistency throughout the entire piece of writing. After learning about paragraphs, students will develop experiment reports, including introductions, methodology, results, and conclusions. They will cite supporting evidence, and make effective deductions. After completing this section, learners should be more competent and confident in writing a well-structured, clearly-written experiment report.

This section covers:

- Format
- Pre-Writing
- Sentences
- Paragraphs
- Experiment Reports

Format

Unless you are specifically told otherwise, you are expected to type and print writing assignments. It is important that the assignment is arranged and presented in an appropriate way, and this is called "format." The format that is presented here is called Institute of Electrical and Electronics Engineers (IEEE) style. Other styles are available.

Activity 1

The following paragraphs are about the history of Sungkyunkwan University. The content is the same, but the format is different. Read the two paragraphs and pay attention to the format. Identify the errors in the first that are corrected in the second.

Sungkyunkwan University (SKKU) was founded in 1398 as a Confucian school for the privileged and upper class.

The original campus is located in what is now Myeongnyun-dong, Seoul. During the Japanese occupation from 1911, the school was renamed Kyonghagwon, and remained so until 1946 when the occupation ended and the original name, Sungkyunkwan, was restored. Over the next three decades, SKKU grew in size and reputation.

Facing an increasing student enrollment, and restricted by limited space around the campus in central Seoul, SKKU expanded its campus in 1978 and developed a second site in suwon that houses natural science, engineering, medicine, and sports departments.

The university currently has an enrollment of around 35,000 students, and together, the two campuses constitute one of Korea's largest centers of learning.

Sungkyunkwan University

Sungkyunkwan University (SKKU) was founded in 1398 as a Confucian school for the privileged and upper class. The original campus is located in what is now Myeongnyun-dong, Seoul. During the Japanese occupation from 1911, the school was renamed Kyonghagwon, and remained so until 1946 when the occupation ended and the original name, Sungkyunkwan, was restored. Over the next three decades, SKKU grew in size and reputation. Facing an increasing student enrollment and restricted by limited space around the campus in central Seoul, SKKU expanded its campus in 1978 and developed a second site in Suwon that houses natural science, engineering, medicine, and sports departments. The university currently has an enrollment of around 35,000 students, and together, the two campuses constitute one of Korea's largest centers of learning.

» Format Guideline

Check

Line space
Set the line spacing to 2 (Ctrl+2 in Microsoft Word).

Title
All writing assignments require a title centered at the top of the first page.
The title should not be a sentence, and it should follow all of the capitalization, font, and size guidelines.

Indent
Indent the first line of the paragraph with the TAB key. (Set indent to 1.27 cm.)

Size
Use font size 12.

Font
Use a plain font such as Times New Roman. Do not use a fancy font.

Margins
Set margins to 2.54 cm in your word processor.

Check
Check your paper for spelling and grammar. Do not make handwritten corrections.

Personal details
Write your full name, class, and student number in the top corner of the first page.

Pre-writing

The aim of pre-writing is to focus thoughts, develop ideas, and explore your topic in preparation for writing. There are a number of methods that can be used in pre-writing.

Free Writing

The aim is to write continuously on the page without stopping to think. Write whatever comes to mind, and do not worry about grammar, spelling, or word choice. It can be done on the computer or on paper. You might start with a general topic (for example, jobs) or a theme (for example, definitive writing), but you can also write completely freely and see what develops.

The keys to effective free writing:
- Set a time limit
- Write for the whole of the allotted time
- Write down everything that comes into your head, regardless of logic or quality

Activity 1

Practice free writing for ten minutes, and then read your work. Were the ideas connected, or did they jump around from topic to topic? Read your partner's work.

List

Listing is a form of brainstorming in which writers list of all the ideas that come to their mind in a set time.

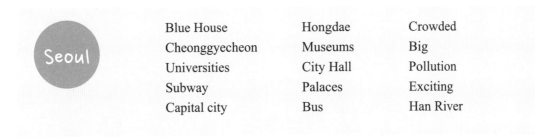

Seoul			
Blue House	Hongdae	Crowded
Cheonggyecheon	Museums	Big
Universities	City Hall	Pollution
Subway	Palaces	Exciting
Capital city	Bus	Han River

Activity 2

In your notebook, list ideas for one of the following topics.

University	Friend	Sport	Hero

Mind Map

A mind map is a great way to organize ideas according to relationships or common features.

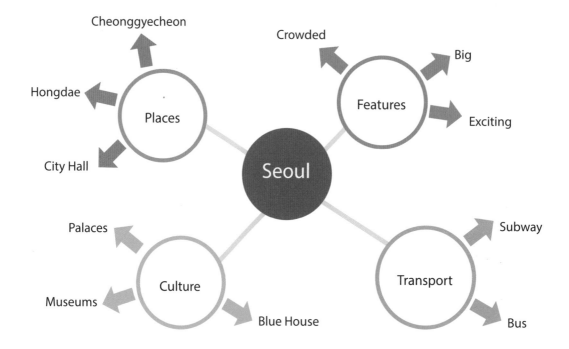

Activity 3

Make a mind map to connect your ideas from Activity 2.

Web Search

These days, the first place people go for ideas is often the Internet. The Internet gives us access to an almost unlimited amount of information, all at our fingertips. While the Internet should not be the only resource, it is a valuable tool.

Activity 4

Use the Internet to research one of the following topics. Use at least three sources.

| Christmas | Chuseok | Easter | Halloween |

Cut and paste the information relevant to the topic into a Word document. Copy the URL for each source onto the document. Each source and its content should be color coded or in a different font. Arrange the information in a logical way so it flows as a single piece. Add a title and list the URLs at the end of the document.

Journal

Many writers keep a journal of thoughts, ideas, and questions. This can be a creative tool for developing ideas for future writing projects.

Activity 5

The methods described in this chapter can be used individually or they can be used together as a longer process. Practice prewriting by following this process.

1. Free write for ten minutes.

2. Take one idea from the free writing section as a topic, and make a list of related ideas.

3. Organize these ideas into a clear, logical mind map.

4. Do a web search on the topic being developed, and gather three good sources.

5. Arrange your ideas and the information from the web search into a logical order.

3 Sentences

A sentence is a complete idea, and it contains a subject and a verb. In other words, a sentence is composed of one or more clauses, which are grammatical units containing at least an explicit or implied subject, and a predicate. Clauses may be independent (IC) or dependent (DC).

What is an Independent Clause?

An independent clause is the part of a sentence that can stand by itself because it includes a subject, verb, and complete idea.

What is a Dependent Clause?

A dependent clause requires an independent clause to make a complete sentence because it is incomplete by itself.

Types of Sentences

Type of Sentence	Sentence Construction
Simple Sentence	One IC
Compound Sentence	More than one IC, no DC
Complex Sentence	One IC, at least one DC
Compound-Complex Sentence	More than one IC, one or more DC

Grammar Tip

Complete Sentences

- Start with a capital letter.
- Finish with a period (.), a question mark (?), or an exclamation mark (!).
- Contain at least one independent clause (IC), which includes a subject (S), a verb (V), and a complete idea.

Capital letter   S   V   V   Period

A sneaky burglar broke into my house and ate all my spaghetti.

                       IC

Capital letter   S   V

London's famous underground "Tube" system is in trouble because the ancient infrastructure was not designed to cope with the demands of modern society.

                                         Period

» Sentence Structure and Variety

Because writers do not want to repeatedly use the same type of sentence structure in their writing, they use different types of sentences to make their writing more effective. This section will help students identify and construct different sentence types.

Simple Sentences and Sentence Fragments

The simple sentence is a single clause that includes a subject, verb, and a complete idea. Simple sentences are also known as independent clauses when they are part of longer sentences. Sentences that are incomplete are called sentence fragments.

Examples:
Simple Sentence: The animal was sick.
Sentence Fragment: Because the animal was sick.

Activity 1

Read the following sentences, and identify the subject and verb in each section. If the sentence is a sentence fragment, finish the sentence yourself.

1. The monkeys were hungry.

2. The massive storm destroyed many of the trees in the jungle.

3. While walking in the jungle.

4. Who gave a lecture on gorillas?

5. Who gave a lecture on gorillas.

6. Because the zoo was closed.

7. The biologist gave the school children a tour of the zoo.

8. The biologist who studies monkeys.

9. The conservation program focuses on preserving natural habitat.

10. After the lecture on preserving natural habitat.

Compound Sentences

Compound sentences are two simple sentences joined by a comma with a coordinating conjunction (FANBOYS). Each coordinating conjunction shows a relationship.

Coordinating Conjunctions	Example
For (cause)	He was late for class, **for** he missed the bus.
And (addition)	She is rich, **and** he likes shopping.
Nor (negative choice)	She did not want help, **nor** did she ask for it.
But (contrast)	She wanted to meet her friends, **but** she had to study.
Or (positive choice)	We can go to Caribbean Bay, **or** we can go to Everland.
Yet (contrast/concession)	He is a heavy smoker, **yet** he is a good athlete.
So (effect)	It rained last weekend, **so** the picnic was canceled.

Punctuation Tip

Commas in Compound Sentences

When joining two independent clauses with a conjunction, a comma (,) is used after the first clause and before the conjunction.

Two simple sentences: Rabbits are plant eaters. Tigers eat meat.
One compound sentence: Rabbits are plant eaters, **but** tigers eat meat.

If the sentence contains only one independent clause and a conjunction, a comma is not used because it is not a compound sentence.

Compound sentence: Rabbits eat grass, **and** rabbits eat weeds.
Simple sentence: Rabbits eat grass and weeds.

Activity 2

Write a "C" (compound) or "NC" (not compound) beside the following sentences.

1. Elephants eat leaves and fruit.
2. Elephants eat leaves, fruit, and grass.
3. Elephants eat leaves, fruit, and grass, but they never eat fish.
4. Bats eat so many different kinds of food.
5. Bears sleep most of the winter, so they are hibernating animals.
6. Bats are active at night, for they are nocturnal animals.
7. Camels have one or two humps on their backs.
8. Neither cats nor dogs live in water.
9. Pandas' bodies are suited for eating meat, yet they eat bamboo.
10. Dolphins cannot live on land, nor can whales live on land.

Complex Sentences

Complex sentences are independent clauses joined by subordinating conjunctions to subordinating (or dependent) clauses. In complex sentences, commas are only used if the dependent clause comes first.

Because their tusks are ivory, elephants are sometimes killed by poachers.
Elephants are sometimes killed by poachers **because** their tusks are ivory.

Subordinating Conjunctions

The following table shows the subordinating conjunctions using "ON A WHITE BUS."

Subordinating Words	Example
Only if	I will cook **only if** you wash the dishes.
Now that	**Now that** I feel better, I can go back to work.
After, although, as	**Although** the fish smelled bad, it tasted good.
When, whenever, where, wherever, while, whereas, whether or not	Julia wore glasses **when** she was young.
If, in case	**If** you leave the room, please lock the door.
Though	**Though** she was angry, she smiled.
Even though, even if	**Even** if you are on a diet, you need to eat.
Because, before	**Before** she became a vegetarian, she loved beef.
Unless, until	**Unless** they hurry up, they will be late.
Since, so that	**Since** he was young, he has loved dogs.

Activity 3

Insert an appropriate subordinating conjunction in the following sentences. In addition, identify the independent and dependent clauses.

1. _____ rats carry diseases, people do not want them in homes.

2. _____ baby birds can fly, their parents bring them food.

3. _____ kangaroos are babies, they live in their mother's pouch.

4. _____ many snakes are harmless, many people are afraid of them.

5. Baby frogs can live on land _____ they grow legs and lungs.

6. Sharks do not attack humans _____ they are hungry.

7. _____ skunks feel in danger, they expel a horrible spray.

8. Kittens cannot open their eyes _____ they are born.

Activity 4

Interview your partner. Take notes of your partner's information in your notebook, and use them to write a mix of compound and complex sentences underneath your notes. Use the following questions as a starting point, but make sure you think of some interesting questions of your own.

1. What musical instrument would you like to learn?
2. Which film star would you like to play you in the movie of your life?
3. What do you look for in a boyfriend or girlfriend?
4. What animal best represents you?
5. Which species of animal would you exterminate?
6. Which household chore is your least favorite?
7. Which country would you never want to visit?
8. Which celebrity would you like to meet?

Punctuation Tip

Joining Independent Clauses with Semicolons and Colons

A semicolon (;) can join two related independent clauses.

Example: Mosquitoes can carry malaria; they are also a dengue fever vector.
The second clause may begin with a transition word followed by a comma.

Example: Mosquitoes are usually harmless; however, they can transmit serious diseases such as malaria and dengue fever.

Independent clauses can also be joined by a colon (:) if the second clause is a deduction from the first, or an explanation or illustration of the first.

Example: The patient was diagnosed with malaria after returning from Madagascar: she probably contracted it while there.

Note that colons after independent clauses have another (unrelated) function: they are also used to introduce lists.

Example: Mosquitoes are vectors for several well-known diseases: malaria, dengue fever, yellow fever, Japanese encephalitis, and Zika fever.

Semicolon Practice

Correct the following sentences by using semicolons.

Example: Mosquitoes carry diseases like malaria; they also transmit dengue fever.

Activity 5

Based on the previous punctuation tip, use semicolons to connect the following sentences.

1. Alligators have sharp teeth. They do not make good pets.

_____

2. Cows are raised for their meat. They are also raised for milk.

_____

3. Chickens have wings. They are not able to fly for long periods.

_____

4. Camels store water in their humps. They can walk long distances without water.

_____

Activity 6

Coordinating conjunctions, subordinating conjunctions, and transition word often convey similar relationships. Using the words given, complete the table.

Coordinating conjunctions: for, and, but, yet, so.

Subordinating conjunctions: while, so that, even though, though, since, due to, because, although

Transitions: nevertheless, because of this, on the other hand, therefore, thus.

Relationship	Words
Addition	
Contrast	
Effect	
Cause	

Activity 7

Rewrite the following sentences in another type of sentence. For instance, try changing a compound sentence into a complex sentence.

Example: Mosquitoes are usually harmless; **however**, they sometimes carry diseases. (;)
Mosquitoes are usually harmless, but they sometimes carry diseases. (compound)
Although mosquitoes are usually harmless, they sometimes carry diseases. (complex)

1. Elephants eat leaves, fruit, and grass, but they never eat fish.

_____

2. Because some rats carry diseases, people do not want them in homes.

_____

3. Bears sleep most of the winter, so they are hibernating animals.

_____

4. Pandas' bodies are suited for eating meat, yet they eat bamboo.

_____

5. Although many snakes are harmless, many people are still afraid of them.

_____

6. Elephants eat leaves and fruit, and they also eat grass.

_____

Compound-Complex

This sentence type combines compound and complex sentences, and/or semicolons into the same sentence. The following simple sentences can be combined into one compound–complex sentence.

Original Passage:

The American Kennel Club recognizes over one hundred and fifty dog breeds. Border Collies are one of the most intelligent breeds. Afghan Hounds are considered one of the least intelligent.

Compound-complex Sentence:

The American Kennel Club recognizes over one hundred and fifty dog breeds, **and** Border Collies are one of the most intelligent dog breeds **while** Afghan Hounds are considered one of the least intelligent.

Activity 8

Use the skills practiced so far to combine the following sentences. Remember to use a variety of sentence types.

1. Pigs are often considered dirty. Pigs do not sweat very much. Pigs cover themselves in mud on hot days to keep cool.

_____

_____

2. Rabbits can have four to twelve babies in each pregnancy. Rabbits are pregnant for thirty days. One rabbit can have eight hundred descendants in nine months.

_____

_____

3. Chameleons have many talents. Chameleons can sleep upside down. Chameleons can change color in reaction to temperature changes. Chameleons' eyes can turn independently of one another.

_____

_____

4. Chimpanzees use tools like sticks to find food. Chimpanzees are very similar to humans. The two species share 98.4% of the same genetic material. Chimpanzees can recognize themselves in a mirror.

_____

_____

5. Many oysters change their sex several times in their lives. Shrimp are born male. Shrimp become female as they get older. Some animals do not have a stable sex.

_____

_____

Comma Splices

Comma splices are incomplete sentences that incorrectly combine independent clauses with a comma.

Example:
Horses can sleep standing up, they can also sleep lying down.

There are four ways to correct comma splices:

1. Use a period after the first independent clause to create two separate sentences.
   Horses can sleep standing up. They can also sleep lying down.

2. Insert a semicolon after the first independent clause to create a compound sentence.
   Horses can sleep standing up; they can also sleep lying down.

3. Insert a coordinating conjunction after the comma to create a compound sentence.
   Horses can sleep standing up, and they can also sleep lying down.

4. Insert a subordinating conjunction at the beginning of the clause to create a complex sentence.
   While horses can sleep standing up, they can also sleep lying down.

Activity 9

Correct the following comma splices.

1. Chickens eat seeds, they also eat small animals like lizards or mice.

_____

2. Sheep are raised for their wool, they are also raised for their milk and meat.

_____

3. Many parrots can learn to speak human languages, they are popular as pets.

_____

4. In some areas, tigers are nearly extinct, they are hunted for their beautiful fur.

_____

5. Turtles appeared about 215 million years ago, they are one of the oldest orders of reptiles.

_____

4 Paragraphs

A paragraph is an organizational unit or chunk in writing that comprises a group of sentences on a single theme or topic. Most writing is organized into themed chunks ranging in length from a single sentence to a dozen or more sentences. Regardless of the length, these chunks should develop the main idea in a clear and logical way.

A paragraph may stand by itself or be one part of a longer piece of work. In scientific writing, paragraphs are often used to answer short questions, give definitions, explain effects, or describe processes. If you can write good paragraphs, you can write good reports. This unit starts with the essentials of paragraph writing and then moves on to how to combine and expand individual paragraphs to build reports.

Paragraph Structure

A good paragraph usually has three basic parts, as shown in the basic outline below.

Title

1. Topic sentence

2. Supporting sentences
  a. Supporting detail
  b. Supporting detail
  c. Supporting detail

3. Concluding sentence

Title: Africa's Most Dangerous Animal

1. Topic sentence

Africa's most dangerous animal is the hippopotamus.

2. Supporting sentences

a. Physical characteristics powerful animal, three meters in length, can weigh over three tonnes, can outrun a human, has powerful jaws that can easily bite a person in half.

b. Temperament - very bad tempered, anyone who gets in between an adult hippopotamus and its calf or the water is likely to be attacked.

c. Statistics – Kills more than 500 people each year, more than any other large African animal.

3. Concluding sentence

The power, temperament, and number of victims of the hippopotamus make it the most feared animal in Africa.

When put together, the pieces create a strong outline for a logical and coherent paragraph.

Africa's Most Dangerous Animal

Africa's most dangerous animal is the hippopotamus. First of all, it is a very powerful animal. It grows up to three meters in length, can weigh over three tonnes, and can outrun a human. It also has extremely powerful jaws that can easily bite a person in half. Secondly, the hippopotamus is very bad tempered. Anyone who gets in between an adult hippopotamus and its calf or the water is likely to be attacked. Finally, the hippopotamus is responsible for more than 500 deaths each year, which is more than any other large African animal. In conclusion, the power, temperament, and number of victims of the hippopotamus make it the most feared animal in Africa.

» The Topic Sentence

What is a topic sentence? The topic sentence can be seen as the key to your paragraph. It is the most important part of the paragraph, and it opens the door to your opinions or ideas about the topic. It gives the reader the main idea and must clearly state what the paragraph is about. As it is usually the first sentence, it must also catch the reader's attention.

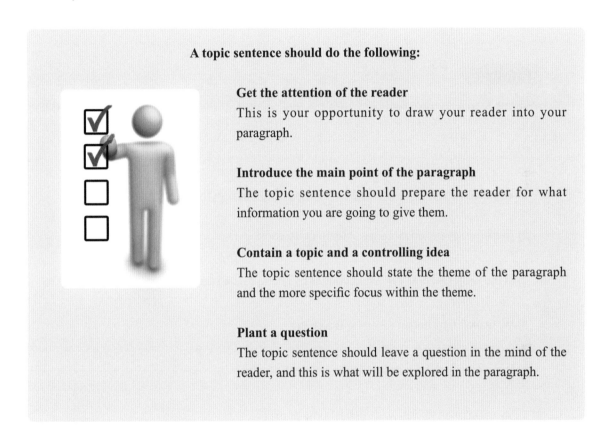

A topic sentence should do the following:

Get the attention of the reader
This is your opportunity to draw your reader into your paragraph.

Introduce the main point of the paragraph
The topic sentence should prepare the reader for what information you are going to give them.

Contain a topic and a controlling idea
The topic sentence should state the theme of the paragraph and the more specific focus within the theme.

Plant a question
The topic sentence should leave a question in the mind of the reader, and this is what will be explored in the paragraph.

A topic sentence has a topic and controlling idea. The topic is the thing being written about, and the controlling idea is the angle or point of focus.

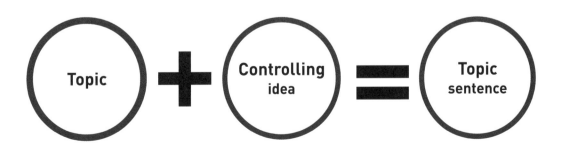

Topic + Controlling idea = Topic sentence

Topic	Controlling idea

Example 1: Apoptosis, or programmed cell death, **has three qualities that make it a potential treatment for cancer.**

Example 2: Despite their similar appearance, there are **several important differences** between **tomato sauce and red pepper paste.**

Topics   Controlling idea

Activity 1

Read the following topic sentences, put the topic in parentheses, and underline the controlling idea.

Example: (Brunel) revolutionized civil engineering through three landmark projects.

1) There are several advantages of learning to cook.

2) In the winter, people can avoid injuries by taking certain precautions.

3) My fear of dogs began when I was a child.

4) There are several disadvantages to online shopping.

5) My vacation in Hawaii was the best time of my life.

What Makes a Good Topic Sentence?

While there is some variation in how writers construct topic sentences, there are some general principles which are often followed.

1. It is a complete idea.

Good example:
Veganism benefits the environment in three ways.

Poor example: An incomplete sentence
There are many benefits.

2. It states a point that needs to be explained or proven.

Good example:
YX's revolutionary new computer is the best on the market.

Poor example: A simple fact
YX developed a new computer.

3. It has one direction.

Good example:
The college entrance exam should be reformed in three specific ways.

Bad example: Two controlling ideas
The college entrance system has benefits and disadvantages.

4. It has an appropriate focus.

Good example:
Social media appears to be causing serious mental health issues for many young people.

Poor example: Too specific
Social media is damaging for young people because it promotes online over offline relationships, contributes to an unhealthy body image, and leads to cyber bullying.

Poor example: Too broad
Since the beginning of time, communication has been essential.

Activity 2

Look at the following topic sentences. For each one, state whether it is a good topic sentence or a poor one.

Example: It happened years ago when we lived on Stanford Road.
Poor topic sentence. No topic.

1. Ostriches are birds.

_____

2. Hiking is one of the best types of exercise.

_____

3. There are three steps to take.

_____

4. What should be done about unemployment?

_____

5. The government should provide a basic income subsidy for all university students.

_____

6. These days, English education is a hot topic in Korea.

_____

7. English is both an easy and difficult language.

_____

8. There are many similarities between the United States and the United Kingdom.

_____

9. In Korea, people do not need a license to ride a bicycle.

_____

10. Steve Jobs's success came from the good decisions he made early in his career.

_____

Activity 3

Read the following paragraph and select the most appropriate topic sentence from the list below.

Peterborough

Topic sentence: _____

First, Peterborough is known for Flagg Fen, which is an ancient Bronze Age settlement. The old town, which dates back to 1365 BCE, is one of the most important places in the country for studying ancient civilizations. The next historic site is Longthorpe, a picturesque village which features a Roman fort from the first century CE. The buildings in the village are all very old and traditional, yet they are all still lived in today. The third and most famous ancient structure is Peterborough Cathedral. Its origins can be traced back to 655 CE, and it has been used as a place of worship since then. The imposing Early English Gothic West Front was built in the 12th century and, with its three huge arches, is unique in style and a very impressive sight. In conclusion, Peterborough's historic sites make it an interesting and important city.

a. Prince William lives in Peterborough, England.

b. The city of Peterborough, England, is known for several historic features.

c. It is a famous city with many old buildings.

d. Let me introduce my hometown, which is old, beautiful, and fantastic.

Activity 4

Create topic sentences for the topics below.

Smoking

_____

Military service

_____

Blood donation

_____

The Introduction Sentence

The first sentence in a paragraph is usually the topic sentence. However, writers sometimes use the opening one or two (or more) sentences to provide background information. Like the topic sentence, the introduction sentence is usually more general than the supporting sentences. Unlike the topic sentence, the introduction sentence is not referred to in or supported by the supporting sentences. In most cases, the introduction sentence gives a general point to introduce the topic and then the topic sentence introduces the main idea which is not mentioned in the introduction sentence.

Activity 5

Read the paragraph below and identify the introduction sentence and the topic sentence.

Africa's Most Dangerous Animal

Africa is a large continent that is well known for its diverse and often dangerous wildlife. Surprisingly, the animal that is considered the most dangerous is the hippopotamus. First of all, the hippopotamus is a very powerful animal. It grows up to three meters in length, can weigh over three tonnes, and can outrun a human. It also has extremely powerful jaws that can easily bite a person in half. Secondly, the hippopotamus is very bad tempered. Anyone who gets in between an adult hippopotamus and its calf or the water is likely to be attacked. Finally, the hippopotamus is responsible for more than 500 deaths each year, which is more than any other large African animal. In conclusion the power, temperament, and number of victims of the hippopotamus make it the most feared animal in Africa.

Activity 6

Write one or two introduction sentences to give background information that will introduce each of the following topic sentences.

Introduction sentence: _____

_____

Topic sentence: Soccer is the greatest team sport in the world.

Introduction sentence: _____

_____

Topic sentence: There are three key steps to a flawless complexion.

» Supporting Sentences

In academic writing, writers must support their ideas. This might well require research and investigation on the part of the writer in order to gather sufficient support. The supporting information in a paragraph is given in the supporting sentences, the sentences that follow the topic sentence. They should always relate to the topic and back up the main idea.

Example: Topic sentence: My cat has three annoying habits.
1. Sleeping on me
2. Shedding fur
3. Leaving dead rodents under the refrigerator

Activity 1

Read the following paragraph and complete the exercises.

Fast Food Phobia

Fast food, particularly McDonald's, is an easy target for people who claim to care about health. However, there are good reasons to believe that McDonald's is not a dietary evil. First of all, there is the assumption that McDonald's meals are fattening due to the high calorie content. In fact, Big Macs contain 510 kcal, far below men's recommended daily intake of 2550 kcal, and women's 1940 kcal. A double quarter pounder with cheese—the most calorific item—has 740 kcal [1]. The second common criticism leveled at McDonald's is the amount of trans-fat. In reality, all meat contains some trans-fat, so the same criticism must also be aimed at every restaurant serving meat. McDonald's burgers contain about 1.5 g of trans-fat per serving, which is just 8 % of the daily limit recommended by the World Health Organization [2]. Finally, the salt—more specifically, sodium—content of McDonald's meals is often considered a major health problem, yet data shows that this criticism is unjustified. The recommended daily intake of sodium for an adult is 1500–2300 mg. A Big Mac, McDonald's most famous and popular burger, contains only 1040 mg of sodium [3], which is well within the healthy limit. In summary, as with any other food, McDonald's can be part of a healthy diet as long as it is eaten in moderation.

1. Underline the topic sentence.

2. What are the three supporting ideas?

a) _____

b) _____

c) _____

Activity 2

Add ideas to support each of the following topic sentences.

There are three important components to the perfect date.

1. _____

2. _____

3. _____

There are several economic advantages to hosting the Olympic Games.

1. _____

2. _____

3. _____

A monarchy serves important functions.

1. _____

2. _____

3. _____

Evidence and Support

Each supporting sentence contains an idea that supports the topic sentence, along with supporting details or evidence to back up the idea. Supporting details are given in the form of examples, statistics, and quotations.

Examples

Examples are the easiest and most common supporting details. They are useful for adding interesting support to a paragraph and do not usually require as much research as quotes and statistics.

> **Example**: Psychology graduates learn a range of skills that are desired by many employers, such as numerical and statistical skills, effective communication skills, and teamwork.

Statistics

Statistics are a good way of giving specific details using numbers. They can be very strong support for a point and can provide detailed and even surprising information.

> **Example**: 28.7 % of psychology graduates are attracted to accountancy, banking, and management, which are growth areas, compared with just 14 % of IT graduates.

Quotations

While quotations are common in the social sciences, humanities, and arts, it is rare to quote in the natural sciences and engineering. Nevertheless, quotes are occasionally used, and the example below shows how this is done in IEEE style.

> **Example**: "The basis for enhanced decision making is the availability of timely and high-quality data." [1]
>
> **Reference**:
> [1]   D. Pivoto, P. D. Waquil, E. Talamini, C. P. S. Finocchio, V. F. Dalla Corte, and G. de Vargas Mores, "Scientific development of smart farming technologies and their application in Brazil," *Inf. Process. Agric.*, vol. 5, no. 1, pp. 21–32, 2018.

Activity 3

Read the paragraph. Identify the relevant supporting sentences. What kind of support does the writer use? Underline any examples, statistics, and quotations.

The Most Employable Graduates

In 2021, almost one in four recent graduates in Korea was unemployed [1]. However, among the most successful may have been psychology graduates due to the skills learned, flexibility of the qualification, and practical experience gained on the course. Psychology graduates learn a range of skills that are desired by many employers, such as numerical and statistical skills, effective communication skills, and teamwork. Second, psychology graduates are often drawn to industries with more vacancies. 28.7 % of psychology graduates are attracted to accountancy, banking, and management, which are growth areas, compared with just 14 % of IT graduates [2]. Finally, it is common for psychology students to gain practical experience in the workplace prior to graduation. Such students know they need at least a year's internship before becoming licensed [3]. Therefore, the skills, versatility, and experience gained by psychology graduates makes them successful in the job market.

References

[1]   Yonhap News, "S. Korea's employment rate of university grads ranks low among OECD: report," Nov. 18, 2021. https://en.yna.co.kr/view/AEN20211118001200320 (accessed Jun. 30, 2022).

[2]   A. White, "What makes psychology and geography grads the most employable?," *The Guardian*, Nov. 18, 2010. https://www.theguardian.com/careers/careers-blog/experts-view-why-are-certain-grads-less-likely-to-be-unemployed (accessed Jun. 30, 2022).

[3]   Careers in Psychology, "10 things to know before becoming a psychologist." https://careersinpsychology.org/ten-things-wish-knew-before-becoming-psychologist/ (accessed Jun. 30, 2022).

Activity 4

Read the paragraph about fast food again (page 29) and summarize the supporting details in the appropriate box.

Example:

Statistic:

Activity 5

Write a topic sentence on the following topics and give three supporting details.

| Sport | Technology | University |

Topic sentence:

_____

Supporting details:

_____

_____

_____

Topic sentence:

_____

Supporting details:

_____

_____

_____

Topic sentence:

_____

Supporting details:

_____

_____

_____

Unity

It is important that all of the supporting sentences in a paragraph match the topic sentence. This means that they should relate to both the topic and the controlling idea. If you are writing a paragraph about the life of Joseph Merrick, then all the supporting sentences should relate directly to the life of Joseph Merrick. Furthermore, each supporting sentence should relate to a single aspect of his life. We should not have sentences that focus on the romantic relationships of Joseph Merrick's sister, or on the pets of Joseph Merrick.

There are two common problems relating to unity in paragraphs.
1. The paragraph contains sentences relating to more than one topic.
2. The paragraph contains sentences supporting more than one controlling idea.

 Tip

For a cohesive paragraph, repeat the key nouns throughout the paragraph. You can also use synonyms to keep the cohesion but add variety.

Activity 6

Read the paragraph below and identify the sentence that does not match the topic sentence. Does the paragraph contain a) more than one topic, or b) more than one controlling idea?

The Difficult Life of Joseph Merrick

Life in 1860s London was tough, but it was particularly difficult for "Elephant Man" Joseph Merrick. Merrick is one of a number of famous disabled people to have a film made about their extraordinary life, along with Cristy Brown (*My Left Foot*, 1989) and Rocky Dennis (*Mask*, 1985). Merrick was born with a severe growth problem meaning that bones on the right side of his body, including skull, ribs, arm, and leg, continued to grow throughout his life. This led to respiratory problems, speech impediments, and, most notably, a physically repulsive appearance. After being abandoned as a child, Merrick was picked up by a backstreet sideshow, where he was cruelly treated by the owner who made money from showing his unusual exhibit to a paying public. Merrick was treated as an animal, and it was assumed from his appearance that he was unintelligent. Eventually, he was rescued by Dr. Fredrick Treves, and they built a relationship together. Dr. Treves studied Merrick's condition but could not cure him. Merrick's condition continued to deteriorate and at the age of 27 he died in his sleep. In conclusion, Joseph Merrick's remarkable story reminds us that there is a person behind every face.

Activity 7

Read the paragraph, and identify the sentence that does not match the topic sentence. Does the paragraph contain a) two topics, or b) more than one controlling idea?

Ancient Seoul

Seoul, the capital of South Korea, has a number of historical sites. The most famous is Gyeongbok Palace, which was the residence of the monarchy until Emperor Yunghui (Sunjong) was dethroned during the Japanese occupation in 1910. Gyeongbok Palace was originally built in 1394 as one of the five great palaces of the Joseon Dynasty and is located in the center of the city. The second famous historical site in Seoul is Joggye Temple (Jogyesa), which has been a place of worship for over 600 years. It is located close to Gyeongbok Palace in the center of Seoul. Gyeongju, the capital of Shilla Dynasty, also contains many historical sites including the distinctive dome-shaped tombs in which the remains of ancient rulers are buried. Another historical site in Seoul is the ancient fortress wall that was built to protect Hanyang, the capital of the Joseon Dynasty. The wall surrounds four mountains, Naksan, Namsan, Bugaksan, and Inwangsan and served to protect the city from invasions. In summary, these are just a few examples of the many historical sites in Seoul.

Connecting Words

Connecting words can be used to show the structure of a paragraph by indicating transitions from one supporting point to another. The table below shows some possible transition signal words and phrases.

Connecting Words and Phrases	
First, First of all, The first …, To begin with	The first idea in a series or sequence
Second, Secondly …	The second idea in a series or sequence
Third, Thirdly …	The third idea in a series or sequence
Next, Then, After that	The next idea in a series
In addition, Furthermore, Moreover	Making a further point
Similarly, Likewise	Comparing a similar idea
In contrast, On the other hand Nevertheless	Showing an opposing idea
Soon, Eventually	A transition over time in a time order paragraph

Activity 8

Read the paragraphs about ancient Seoul and Joseph Merrick once more and identify the connecting words and phrases.

Activity 9

Use the facts in the box below to create a series of supporting sentences on the topic below. Write a topic sentence to which all of your supporting sentences relate.

Ben Folds Five Facts

Career: Formed in 1993, broke up in 2000

Albums and chart success: *Ben Folds Five* (1995), did not chart in US Billboard 200

Whatever and Ever Amen (1997), reached no. 42 in US Billboard 200

The Unauthorized Biography of Reinhold Messner (1999), reached no. 35 in US Billboard 200

Members: Ben Folds (piano, vocals), Robert Sledge (bass guitar, vocals), Darren Jessee (drums, vocals)

From: North Carolina, USA

Most successful single: "Brick" (1997), reached no.19 in US Hot 100 Billboard Chart

Genre: Alternative rock

Known for: No guitar, songs that tell stories

Topic: _____

Title: _____

Topic sentence:

_____

Supporting sentences: _____

_____

_____

_____

_____

_____

_____

Activity 10

Now do the same but with details from your own research.

Topic: _____

Title: _____

Topic sentence:

_____

_____

_____

_____

Supporting sentences:

_____

_____

_____

_____

_____

_____

_____

_____

_____

_____

_____

_____

_____

_____

_____

_____

_____

_____

» The Concluding Sentence

The concluding sentence is the final sentence in a paragraph. It finishes the paragraph in a satisfying way, and it helps the reader to cement their understanding of the ideas.

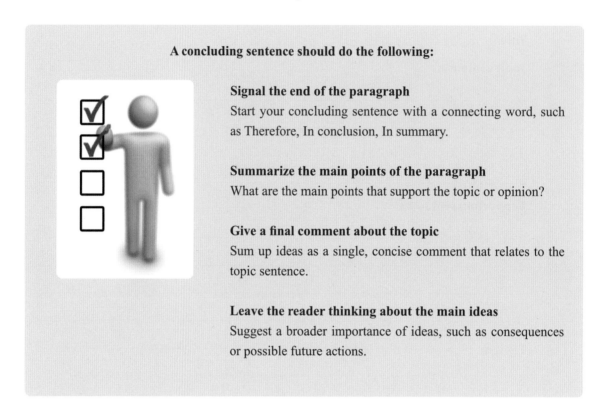

A concluding sentence should do the following:

Signal the end of the paragraph
Start your concluding sentence with a connecting word, such as Therefore, In conclusion, In summary.

Summarize the main points of the paragraph
What are the main points that support the topic or opinion?

Give a final comment about the topic
Sum up ideas as a single, concise comment that relates to the topic sentence.

Leave the reader thinking about the main ideas
Suggest a broader importance of ideas, such as consequences or possible future actions.

What Makes a Good Concluding Sentence?

Most paragraphs end with a concluding sentence. This sentence either reinforces the controlling idea, or leaves readers with a related thought. All concluding sentences need to address the following points.

1. It signals the end of the paragraph.

It is helpful to start the concluding sentence with a clear signal that this is the end of the paragraph. This shows the reader that there will be no new information, and that the main point of the paragraph is about to be restated. These signals are typically *summations* or *transitions*.

Summation		Transition	
	In conclusion,		Therefore,
	To sum up,		Thus,
	In summary,		As a result,
	To summarize,		Consequently,
	In brief,		The evidence shows that
	In short,		It is clear that
	From this, we can conclude that…		We have seen that…
			While it is true that…,

The way that the paragraph ends depends on the type of paragraph. For example, a definition paragraph may end by summarizing the main details.

2. Conclude the paragraph in one of four ways.

a. Restate the topic sentence
Paraphrase the topic and controlling idea to reinforce the basic point of the paragraph.
Concluding Sentence: People love cats for their many endearing qualities.

b. Restate the topic sentence and three major details
Paraphrase the main points of the paragraph to reinforce the main message.
Concluding Sentence: In conclusion, people feel great affection for cats because of their devotion, cleverness, and friendliness.

c. Make a related suggestion
Suggest a course of action to the reader based on the point of the paragraph.
Concluding Sentence: In summary, if people want an animal with an interesting personality, they should get a cat.

d. Make a related prediction

Write something that will happen in the near future based on the point of the paragraph.

Concluding Sentence: As a result, people will fall in love with cats' appealing characteristics if they become cat owners.

Tip

Do not put any new information in your concluding sentence.

Do not leave a personal message to the reader.

Activity 1

Read the following paragraph and use what you have learned so far to select the most appropriate concluding sentence from the options.

Ig Nobels

The Ig Nobels, an event that recognizes ingenuity in science research, is an awards ceremony like no other. The awards ceremony is organized by Annals of Improbable Research (AIR), which is a humor magazine presented as a parody of serious scientific literature. The self-stated aim of the Ig Nobels is "first make people laugh, and then make them think." Each year in October, scientists gather for the annual Ig Nobel awards ceremony, held at Harvard University, to see prizes distributed by genuine Nobel Prize winners. As with many awards ceremonies, the Ig Nobel prize winners are expected to make a speech, and the organizers have implemented an unusual but effective method for keeping these speeches from going on for too long. Miss Sweety Poo is a young girl who sits on the stage and as soon as she is tired of a speech repeats, "Please stop: I'm bored," until the speaker leaves the stage. While the ceremony is known for rewarding unusual research, there is often a use for the findings. For example, a study showing that malaria mosquitoes are attracted to the smell of human feet, and also, Limburger cheese has led to the development of effective mosquito traps. However, bad science is also recognized and rewarded as a criticism, such as with Jacques Benveniste. Benveniste's research "proved" that water has a memory, and that this information can be transmitted over the Internet.

_____

_____

a) While science is often seen as serious, the Ig Nobels give a more lighthearted angle focused on humor and entertainment.

b) In summary, the Ig Nobel awards are the biggest prizes in the science community.

c) In conclusion, the Ig Nobels are an unusual ceremony that began in 1991.

d) Furthermore, the unusual nature of the Ig Nobel awards makes them one of the highlights of the science calendar.

Types of Concluding Sentences

There are two main types of concluding sentences. The first is a summary of the main points of the paragraph while the second restates the topic sentence in different words.

Activity 2

Read the paragraph about the evolution of snakes.

1. Identify the topic sentence.

2. Identify the supporting details. How do they support the topic sentence?
   Then read the two example concluding sentences and identify which one is a summary of the main points of the paragraph and which is a restatement of the topic sentence.

Legless

Occasionally venomous, often depicted as cunning or deceitful, one thing that all snakes have in common is, besides their tail, an obvious absence of limbs. However, the evidence suggests that this has not always been the case. Experts believe that all lizards and snakes evolved from a reptilian common ancestor. Fossil evidence from the Cretaceous Period (144–65 million years ago) reveals at least four genera of early snakes: three in the Middle East and one in South America. The unusual feature of these snake fossils is the presence of short hind legs. These early snakes evolved from burrowing lizards with short and stubby limbs, and streamlined bodies. Over time, the front legs regressed until they were just short vestigial stumps. Fossils of primitive species, such as boas and pythons, still have these vestigial stumps as evidence of their legged ancestors. These are known as anal spurs and are used to grip during mating. Other modern snake species have lost even these traces of their lizard heritage. Genetic evidence reveals that evolution in Hox genes, which are responsible for limb development, resulted in the dramatic reduction on limb size and the eventual loss of functioning front and hind limbs in all modern snakes.

_____

_____

Concluding sentence 1: In conclusion, various lines of evidence show that primitive snakes had legs.

Concluding sentence 2: It is clear from fossil evidence, the anatomy of primitive modern snake species, and genetic analysis, that legless modern snakes evolved from legged ancestors.

Activity 3

There are four main steps in the process of writing a concluding sentence.

Step 1: Underline the topic sentence.

Step 2: Highlight the supporting ideas.

Step 3: Start the concluding sentence with a connecting word.

Step 4: Choose a type of concluding sentence.

Choosing a Pet

There are a number of things to consider when choosing a pet. Most importantly, people must carefully consider whether or not they are really ready to take on the responsibility of caring for an animal. Can they provide a pet with everything it will need in order to live a happy life in their care? Once someone is sure they can handle a pet, they must think about what they want from their pet. Fish look beautiful and are not too demanding in terms of time and space, but some consider them boring. Dogs and cats can be playful, affectionate, and can become great companions. Hamsters are popular and cute, but they are nocturnal. Some people want a more unusual pet, such as a lizard or an axolotl which need specialist equipment and knowledge. Finally, anyone thinking of buying a pet must consider what they are able to offer their animal. For someone with ample time and space, a dog might be a great option since they need exercise and attention. For someone who has never kept a pet before, it might be a good idea to start with a rabbit, which does not require training and does not live as long. It is irresponsible to get a pet which people cannot care for adequately.

Concluding sentence:

_____

_____

Activity 4

Read the following topic sentences from paragraphs elsewhere in the chapter, and rewrite them as concluding sentences.

Seoul, the capital of South Korea, has a number of historical sites.

_____

_____

_____

_____

Life in 1860s London was tough, but it was particularly difficult for "Elephant Man" Joseph Merrick.

_____

_____

_____

_____

Among the most successful employees were psychology graduates due to the skills learned, flexibility of the qualification, and practical experience gained on the course.

_____

_____

_____

_____

Despite the bad press, there are good reasons to reject the widely held belief that McDonald's is a dietary evil.

_____

_____

_____

_____

» Paragraph Outlines

An outline is a useful stage of the planning process in any kind of academic or formal writing, including paragraphs, essays, and reports. It helps you to arrange your ideas in a logical way, and it makes the process of writing your final piece far simpler.

Topic: International Marriage

Topic sentence: In an increasingly globalized society, it is easier than ever before to meet people of other nationalities, and for the benefits to society, international couples, and their children, people should pursue intercultural romance and marriage.

Supporting detail 1: International marriage benefits the couple.

Supporting detail 2: International marriages will benefit society in the long term.

Supporting detail 3: International marriage benefits the children.

Concluding sentence: International relationships should be strongly encouraged.

Activity 1

Here are the components of an outline for a paragraph about yoga. Put them into a logical order by matching them with the relevant paragraph sections.

a. The Benefits of Yoga	1. Topic a
b. Develops clear thinking, improves concentration.	2. Topic sentence: _____
c. Physical benefits.	3. Supporting point 1: _____
d. Reduces fear, anger and worry, helps you to feel calm, develops self-confidence.	4. Detail: _____
e. Mental benefits.	5. Supporting point 2: _____
f. Improves blood circulation, improves digestion, makes you strong and flexible.	6. Detail: _____
g. Emotional benefits.	7. Supporting point 3: _____
h. Therefore, to build mental, physical and emotional health, consider practicing yoga.	8. Detail: _____
i. Practicing yoga regularly can be good for your mind, your body and your emotions.	9. Concluding sentence: _____

Once the supporting points have been arranged in a logical order, you can begin to add details. At this point your paragraph really begins to take shape.

Topic: International Marriage

Topic sentence: In an increasingly globalized society, it is easier than ever before to meet people of other nationalities, and for the benefits to society, international couples, and their children, people should pursue intercultural romance and marriage.

Supporting detail 1: International marriage benefits the couple directly. The couple can learn each other's language and culture, as well as enjoy frequent travel opportunities.

Supporting detail 2: International marriages benefit society in the long term. The resulting increased genetic diversity causes an increase not only in children's intelligence, but also in their lung capacity (forced expiratory capacity [1]), which correlates with physical health (β=1.64, p<0.0011), and healthy social relationships (β=1.21, p<0.0024) [2].

Supporting detail 3: International marriage benefits the children. Children of international parents have the advantage of identifying with two cultures, leading to more rounded opinions and richer life experience.

Concluding sentence: International relationships are nothing new and for the good of couples, society, and children, they are something that should be strongly encouraged.

References:

[1]   P. K. Joshi *et al.*, "Directional dominance on stature and cognition in diverse human populations," *Nature*, vol. 523, pp. 459–462, 2015.

[2]   Y. Wen, D. Wang, M. Zhou, Y. Zhou, Y. Guo, and W. Chen, "Potential effects of lung function reduction on health-related quality of life," *Int. J. Environ. Res. Public Health*, vol. 16, no. 2, 2019.

Activity 2

Add controlling ideas to the following topics to form topic sentences then add three supporting points.

Popular Foreign Food

Topic sentence:

_____

_____

Support 1: _____

Support 2: _____

Support 3: _____

Future Technology

Topic sentence:

_____

_____

Support 1: _____

Support 2: _____

Support 3: _____

Travel Experience

Topic sentence:

_____

_____

Support 1: _____

Support 2: _____

Support 3: _____

Activity 3

Choose one of the topics from Activity 2 and develop it into a paragraph outline.

Topic: _____

_____

Topic sentence: _____

_____

a) Supporting detail 1:

_____

_____

_____

b) Supporting detail 2:

_____

_____

_____

c) Supporting detail 3:

_____

_____

_____

Concluding sentence:

_____

_____

_____

_____

_____

Activity 4

Write a paragraph about one of the topics below within 30 minutes. Start by brainstorming to gather and develop your ideas. Write an outline including a topic sentence, supporting details and a concluding sentence. Finally, write your paragraph.

Hometown	Disaster	Hobby

Plan your time: When writing within a time limit it is very important that you plan your time effectively. Here is a suggestion for planning your time for this writing task.

Brainstorm	5 minutes
Outline	7 minutes
Paragraph	15 minutes
Check	3 minutes

Paragraph checklist: Does your paragraph include the following:

Title	____
Format (see page 10)	____
Topic sentence	____
Relevant supporting details	____
Concluding sentence	____

Activity 5

Using what you have learned so far, write a paragraph on one of the topics below.

An interesting instrument	A common superstition
The perfect partner	A hero
A successful company	Technology of tomorrow

_____

_____

_____

_____

_____

_____

_____

_____

_____

_____

_____

_____

_____

_____

_____

_____

_____

_____

5 Experiment Reports

» Overview

Experiments reports explain the background, purpose, method, and results of research, and interpret the results to draw conclusions. The research is presented in a standard, organized structure so the reader can understand the experiment, and how it was conducted in detail. The report is an archive of the experiment for future researchers to develop. It is clearly structured, so readers may focus only on certain sections, choosing not to read the whole report from the beginning to the end.

Every academic discipline (e.g., chemistry, engineering, medicine) has its own standard organization for presenting research. Authors must be aware of the most commonly used sections of experiment reports in their field. The following are the most common sections across disciplines.

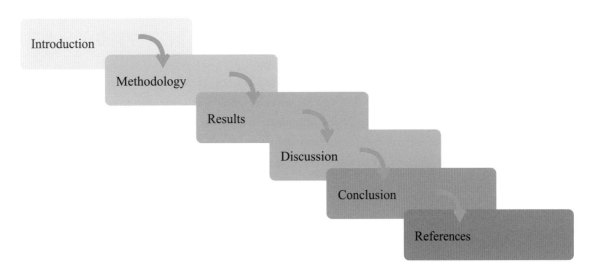

In this section you will:
- examine a model experiment report
- analyze the structure of experiment reports
- develop appropriate grammar for this genre
- write an experiment report.

Answer the following questions with a partner. Share your answers with the class.

1. Why do people publish research?

2. Where can we find published research?

3. Read the following experiment report. What is the purpose of the report?

The Effect of a Diamond Cubic Polypropylene Straw Structure on Protecting Duck Eggs from Impact

1. Introduction

Within the global supply chain, packaging and transport of delicate objects is essential for business. Packaging should often be small and light, with maximal protective capabilities, so research in this field is important to many industries. A common introduction to protecting delicate objects is commonly known as the Egg Drop Experiment. This often features in school curricula to introduce students to fundamental concepts such as gravity, energy, acceleration, mass, and impact, to encourage creativity in experimental design, to foster problem solving skills, and to facilitate understanding of the role of engineering and design [1]. Egg drop parameters often vary in conditions such as size, weight, materials, and durability [2].

One common material used in egg drop experiments is the fast food drinking straw. This thin, light tube of polypropylene is cheap and easily available [3]. It is also versatile as straws can be cut to any length, and the apparatus housing the egg can be constructed in a variety of shapes and patterns. Truss systems are structural patterns that form a rigid design, and when combined, they prevent compression. Diamond—one of the hardest natural materials—is a naturally-occurring example of such structures. Diamond atoms' crystalline arrangement is known as a diamond cubic structure [4 p. 2.16]. This structure links multiple tetrahedra (polyhedra [three-dimensional shapes] composed of four equilateral triangles) at nodes, forming a cubic shape as the tetrahedra link at all nodes.

Though there is great variation and versatility in egg drop experiments, almost all such experiments typically test various structures' protection of chicken eggs since these eggs are widely available. A great amount of more advanced research is based on these fundamental experiments, but it is important to determine structures' protection of a wider range of objects. This experiment therefore aims to determine whether polypropylene straws arranged in a diamond cubic pattern can protect a duck egg from impact on a hard surface after being dropped from a three-story building. The results of this experiment may help industrial designers to determine whether their findings in similar experiments may be more generalizable.

2. Methodology

Twelve duck eggs (mean mass 65.71 g, length 64.77 mm, width 43.93 mm), 100 clear polypropylene drinking straws (diameter 6.09 mm), and clear sticky tape (width 12 mm) were prepared. Straws were cut to 24 mm lengths, and were assembled radially, with sticky tape joining one end of each straw at the same point. The other ends of the straws formed the points of a regular tetrahedron (Fig. 1a). Four such units were linked to form the points of a larger composite tetrahedron—a diamond cubic cell (Fig. 1b). Twenty-seven such cells were constructed, the egg was placed tightly in the space in the center of one cell, and the cells were linked to form a 3×3×3 apparatus of diamond cubic cells with the egg held in the central cell (Fig. 1c). In total, twelve such 3×3×3 apparatuses were constructed, each containing one duck egg.

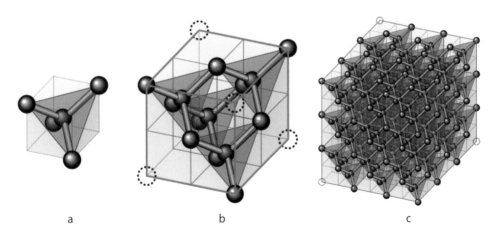

a   b   c

Fig. 1. (a) Single tetrahedron. (b) Larger composite tetrahedron. (c) 3×3×3 apparatus of diamond cubic cells

The egg drops were conducted from a window 9.15 m above a concrete impact site. On the day of testing, the wind speed was reported as 3 m/s, which was considered too negligible to affect results. The units were dropped from a resting position at arm's length from the window while being held centrally at the top. The impact of the apparatus was video recorded at 240 frames per second (fps) and 1080 progressive scan (1080 p) on an iPhone 13 Pro using iOS software version 15.3.1, placed 50 cm from the impact site. The descents were also recorded at 240 fps and 1080 p from the third-floor window with a

Galaxy S22 running Android 12.0 in order to measure the units' rotation while falling.

3. Results

Twelve duck eggs were dropped in this experiment, and results were recorded (Table I). Eleven remained apparently undamaged, but one sustained a visible 16 mm crack. The video footage showed a mean time from drop to impact of 1.31 s. The units rotated mid-air by a mean of 22°, and impacted on a corner each time. There was mild distortion of the diamond cubic apparatus upon impact. A mean of 2.92 straws broke on impact, yet the truss system absorbed the impact, distributing forces horizontally and vertically. The eggs remained encased inside the diamond cubic apparatus without any contact with the ground. No movement was observed in the eggs' positioning while encased in the middle cell.

TABLE I

OBSERVATIONS FROM EGG DROPS

Egg	Crack length (mm)	Straws broken	Descent time (s)	Rotation (°)
1	0	3	1.37	25
2	0	0	1.30	2
3	0	4	1.29	18
4	0	4	1.40	29
5	0	2	1.31	17
6	0	3	1.29	34
7	16	3	1.30	31
8	0	4	1.29	22
9	0	4	1.28	29
10	0	0	1.36	25
11	0	5	1.28	15
12	0	3	1.30	19
Mean (s.d.)	1.33 (4.62)	2.92 (1.56)	1.31 (0.04)	22.17 (8.74)

4. Discussion

These results suggest that at each of the straw nodes, compressional forces distributed impact forces through the straws, away from the egg. It appears likely that the crack sustained by one egg resulted from being held too tightly between straws, suggesting that straw length may need to be revised for different sizes of egg. The diamond cubic structure of straws thus broadly appears to protect duck eggs from impact on a concrete surface after a free fall of approximately 9 m. These results are similar to those typically found with chicken eggs, suggesting that findings may be generalized.

5. Conclusion

This experiment was conducted to determine whether duck eggs would be protected by a diamond cubic crystal structure of triangular straw units when dropped from a height of 9.15 m. In most of the twelve drops, the egg remained intact, though one egg cracked slightly. The rigid durability of a diamond cubic truss system thus appears to absorb kinetic energy, using compressional forces to disperse impact forces. Thus, when an object must withstand an impact by minimizing force absorption, such as in the egg drop project, a diamond cubic structure may successfully encase the structure. It is recommended that future experiments consider a broader range of egg sizes, and that structure size be varied to determine how large apparatuses need to be to protect objects of a range of masses.

6. References

[1] National Committee on Science Education Standards and Assessment, National Research Council, 1996, *National Science Education Standards*, National Academy Press, Washington DC, pp. 161–166

[2] "Soft Landing," pgskids.org, [Online]. Available: https://dsassets.pbskids.org/diy/DSN_NASA_MissionSolarSystem_SoftLanding_Student.pdf [Accessed July 18, 2019]

[3] M. Rober, *1st place Egg Drop project ideas using Science*, 2015, Accessed July 18, 2019. [Streaming Video]. Available: https://youtu.be/nsnyl8llfH4

[4] V. Rajendran, *Materials Science*. Tata McGraw-Hill Pub. 2004.

[5] Cmglee, "Visualisation diamond cubic," *Wikimedia Commons*, Sep. 08, 2013. https://commons.wikimedia.org/wiki/File:Visualisation_diamond_cubic.svg (accessed Jun. 23, 2022).

» Introduction

The introduction provides background information and the objective (aim) of the experiment. Background information gives the reader a general understanding of the experiment's context. The statement of the objective is essential because the experiment results may differ from expectations. The researcher hopes that the objectives will be achieved; however, in many experiments, the results may differ from expectations or hopes. These findings are discussed in the Results section.

Introductions should:

• give background information about the topic (the big picture),
• establish the importance of the experiment (zooming in), and
• introduce the objective (information most specifically about this experiment).

When writing the introduction, pay attention to the grammatical tense. Sentences are typically written in the present simple or present perfect tense to convey general established knowledge.

Giving Background Information

Introducing the reader to the broad context of the experiment is important from the beginning. It gives them background knowledge, and connects the readers' understanding of the issues to the significance of the experiment. It addresses the "big picture", and how the research objective solves or supports this field.

One method of providing background information is the "Funnel Approach." The funnel begins with general opening statements and factual data about the broad context of the topic. Gradually, the information becomes narrower and more focused. The funnel ends with a specific statement that leads the reader into the experiment's objective. It illustrates the underlying motivation, thus showing the reader the big picture.

Establishing the Importance of the Experiment

After understanding the broader context of the experiment, the reader needs to understand how the experiment fits into recent research. Many experiments continue or modify research that has already been published and recognized by the scientific community. By understanding the broad context and similar experiments, readers will become aware of how the experiment is different, and how it has a different perspective. Some questions to consider are:

• What did those experiments not address?
• How does your experiment push research forward?

This approach is known as "Zooming In".

Introducing the Objective

Now that the reader understands the "big picture" and significance of the experiment, state the experiment's objective. Be specific about the conditions and scope of the experiment. This determines how your experimental objective is distinct from previous experiments. Bear in mind that not all experiments are successful, or turn out as expected. It is therefore important to state the motivations which led to the experiment.

The tips below can help in forming an effective objective.

1. Use either past simple or present simple grammar.
2. Use the infinitive form of the verb (e.g., *to determine, to analyze*).
3. Use modal verbs to illustrate the value of the objective.
4. Write the objective as a statement which shows no researcher subjectivity. To help achieve this, avoid personal pronouns such as *I*.
5. Write a brief, detailed objective to give the reader the specific scope of the study.
6. Follow up after the objective to suggest the significance of the study.

Example:

This experiment aims to determine whether 5 mm-thick titanium casing can protect an aircraft's flight recorder from impact in the event of a freefall from an altitude of 10,000 m. The results of this experiment will help manufacturers to minimize recorder weight and production cost while meeting legal requirements.

Activity 1

Review "The Effect of a Diamond Cubic Polypropylene Straw Structure on Protecting Duck Eggs from Impact" (pp. 52–55).

1. How do the authors employ the "Funnel Approach" in the first two paragraphs?

2. What terms or ideas establish the significance of the experiment?

3. Underline the objective of the experiment.

Activity 2

Look at the following experimental objectives. Do you think they are good or need improvement? Rewrite the sentences which need improvement.

1. The purpose of this experiment is to examine whether smoking 10 m away from building entrances is bad for people.

_____

_____

_____

_____

_____

2. The dormitory curfew must be abolished, and I can prove it.

_____

_____

_____

_____

_____

3. Students are able to remember and recall information longer when they enroll in a 9 a.m. class.

_____

_____

_____

_____

_____

4. The objective of this study is to determine the optimum amount of sleep that the average university student needs to optimize their life pattern and to maintain academic achievement.

_____

_____

_____

_____

5. The objective of this study is to determine the psychological factors which would motivate campus students to use reusable instead of disposable drinks containers.

_____

_____

_____

_____

_____

6. We decided to investigate whether exercising helps to improve students' ability to memorize patterns and to recall information over a long period of time.

_____

_____

_____

_____

_____

_____

Activity 3

The following are topics of common superstitions in Korea. Your group wants to test the validity of these superstitions. Write an objective which introduces an experiment.

Example: This study examines the success of athletes depending on whether they follow superstitions.

1. Presenting new shoes to your significant other

_____
_____
_____

2. Electric house fans turned on while sleeping at night

_____
_____
_____

3. Writing names in red ink

_____
_____
_____

4. Whistling at night

_____
_____
_____

5. Eating *miyeok-guk* (seaweed soup)

_____
_____
_____

Activity 4

Read the following objective about drinking coffee after lunch. Imagine that you are the researcher. Use your experience to give background information about coffee consumption, especially in a Korean context, and apply the "Funnel Approach" to reduce the scope before establishing the importance of this experiment.

Provide Background Information:

_____

_____

_____

_____

_____

_____

Establish the Importance of the Experiment:

_____

_____

_____

_____

_____

Introduce the Objective:

The purpose of this article is to present the psychological effects of the consumption of an Americano after consuming a Korean lunch, which typically consists of meat, vegetables, and rice. The participants' mood, mental performance, and hormone levels will be reviewed and discussed. The results of this study will help Korean people to determine whether to consume an Americano after lunch or to forego the caffeinated drink and its stimulating effects.

Activity 5

Read the following background information. If you were the researcher, what would you think the experiment objective was? How would you 'zoom in' to establish the importance of the experiment?

While the South Korean government has taken measures to warn citizens about the health effects of smoking, the average smoking rate remains above 20 percent. In 2006, it was estimated that Korean male smoking deaths constituted 38–40 percent of all male deaths in the 45–70 age group. Although the smoking rate remains lower among Korean females, this has largely been attributed to historical stigmatization of female smoking—it has been largely frowned upon and construed as masculine behavior since the 1880s [1, p. 109]. In January 2015, the government increased the tax on cigarettes by an average of 2,000 won per pack to reduce the smoking rate [2]. In addition, sensational images of the damaging effects of smoking now cover cigarette boxes. However, as people have adjusted to higher prices and the steady pace of inflation, neither initiatives have had a strong impact on reducing the high number of smokers. It appears that further government measures are needed to tax cigarettes out of typical consumers' price range.

References

[1]   A. Lankov, *North of the DMZ: Essays on Daily LIfe in North Korea*. Jefferson, NC: McFarland, 2007.

[2]   S. E. Choi, "Impact of 2015 Korean cigarette tax increase on lower income people," *J. Addict. Res. Ther.*, vol. 8, no. 1, p. 306, 2017.

Establish the Importance of the Experiment:

_____

_____

_____

_____

_____

_____

_____

_____

_____

_____

_____

_____

Introduce the Objective:

_____

_____

_____

_____

_____

_____

_____

_____

_____

_____

_____

_____

» Methodology

The methodology section explains in detail how the experiment was performed. The author provides information about the materials and equipment that were used. Explanation of the experiment helps the reader to question or confirm the validity of the methods that were used. Fundamentally, the experiment should be replicable; i.e., other researchers should be able to emulate the experimental steps, and reach a similar conclusion.

- Describe the step-by-step procedure of the experiment.
- Avoid jargon, and write clearly.
- Don't use personal pronouns such as *I*, e.g. "I put A into B." Use the passive voice instead, e.g., "A was put into B."

Sentences in the methodology section are usually in the past tense since the experiment has already finished when you write the report. This section should not use bullet points to list the steps, and all sentences should be complete sentences.

Activity 1

Review "The Effect of a Diamond Cubic Polypropylene Straw Structure on Protecting Duck Eggs from Impact" (pp. 52–55).

1. What materials did the researchers prepare?

_____

_____

_____

2. Underline the verbs. What grammatical tense are they in?

_____

_____

_____

Tips for Writing Your Methods Section:

- Use the past tense. (Remember that the experiment has already finished.)
- Avoid personal pronouns and personal possessive adjectives (e.g., *I, me, my, you, your*).
- Write in the passive voice. (It is considered more objective.)
- For conciseness, combine simple steps into one sentence.

Activity 2

Rewrite the following three steps using the above tips.

1. First, you prepare a beaker of mixed salt water solution.

2. Then you boil the salt water solution for five minutes.

3. You can then filter the precipitate that has formed through filter paper.

_____

_____

_____

_____

_____

_____

_____

Activity 3

Fix the order of the steps, and rewrite them correctly in the space below.

Removing Caffeine from Coffee Beans

1. The beans were returned to the mixture to absorb the flavor that they lost during the process.

2. The water was kept at this temperature for five hours.

3. The resulting mixture was then heated to evaporate the ethyl acetate and the caffeine.

4. The beans were placed in water, and boiled at 100 °C.

5. The water was then separated, and the beans were moved to another beaker, where they were washed for ten hours with ethyl acetate.

_____

_____

_____

_____

_____

_____

_____

_____

_____

_____

Activity 4

Watch a smartphone drop test video online. Write down the steps in order, explaining how the drop test experiment was conducted. What are the experimental conditions? Use descriptive details to "paint a picture" for readers who have not seen the video. Pay attention to the grammatical tense.

Example: On a clear, sunny day, the performer stood outside on a dry asphalt parking lot surface.

1. _____

2. _____

3. _____

4. _____

5. _____

Activity 5

1. Imagine you are conducting the egg drop experiment from the third floor of a building. List cheap and accessible materials that someone might use to preserve the egg's integrity (to prevent it from breaking). Any materials or objects can be used.

_____

_____

_____

2. Briefly explain how to make or design the egg drop apparatus which will prevent your egg from cracking on impact from a third floor drop.

3. Would your experiment impose any restrictions (e.g., size, weight, durability) on the materials?

Activity 6

Using the information from Activity 5, write a detailed paragraph explaining the methodology of your egg drop experiment. Explain it in a detailed manner to "paint a picture." The readers should understand the steps in detail to replicate the experiment themselves.

_____

_____

_____

_____

_____

_____

_____

_____

_____

_____

_____

_____

_____

_____

» Results

The results section explains the outcomes of the experiment, which may or may not match expectations. The data should reflect the objectives or aim of the experiment conclusively. The authors may also discuss and interpret the outcomes in relation to the experimental objectives. This section is usually the shortest, and it includes an interpretation of the experimental data. From an experimental viewpoint, it is the most important section of the report. It is commonly presented through text, tables, and figures.

- State the results objectively.
- Present results in tables and/or figures.

Activity 1

Review "The Effect of a Diamond Cubic Polypropylene Straw Structure on Protecting Duck Eggs from Impact" (pp. 52–55). Which results do the authors discuss?

_____

_____

_____

Present Selected Sets of Results

Experimenters collect a wide set of data points for their research; however, not all of this raw data will be relevant for confirming or rejecting the experimental objective. In this section, the authors should select the most relevant sets of data, and comment on significant results.

Data should be presented in a visual method such as a table, chart, graph, diagram, or another way which best illustrates the results. The presented data should be solid evidence from the experiment that can be examined and criticized. The visual data presentations should be clear to the reader, and should highlight only the most relevant data, excluding the full raw data.

💡 **Tips for Presenting Visuals:**

- Data should only be labeled as either a table or a figure.
- All visuals presented in the results must be referenced in the comments.
- The visuals have to follow the comments. Tables and figures cannot be presented before being introduced.
- Data or information that is irrelevant to the objective must not be presented.

Example

The study found that Species A grew to a mean height of 15 cm—significantly taller than Species B in Condition X ($p<0.01$). In Condition Y, however, both species grew to a similar height.

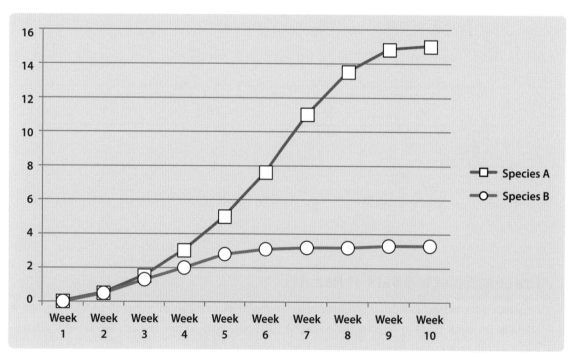

Fig. 1. Plant heights (cm) in Condition X

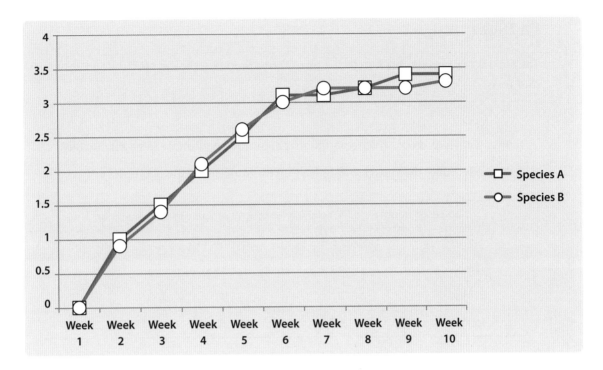

Fig. 2. Plant heights (cm) in Condition X

Activity 2

The table below presents the results of a smartphone drop test. Look at the data, and answer the questions.

1. After numerous drops, which smartphones appear to be the most and least durable?

2. What effect does the impact surface have on the durability of the phones?

Number of drops from a 1m height before the smartphone failed to power on			
Surface	Smartphone X	Smartphone Y	Smartphone Z
Wood	40	50	25
Linoleum	75	80	45
Concrete	8	10	2

3. Next, state the results of the above 'Drop Test Experiment.' Comment on the data, and explain the results.

_____

_____

_____

_____

_____

_____

_____

_____

Activity 3

Fig. 1 presents the percentage of male and female smokers in South Korea.

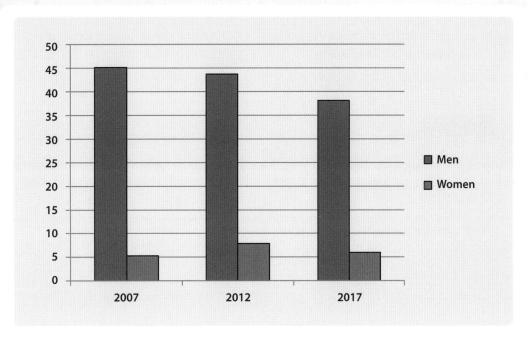

Fig. 1. Percentages of male and female smokers over 19 years old in South Korea [1]

Explain the results illustrated in the above figure. Comment on the data, and explain the results.

_____

_____

_____

_____

_____

Reference

[1]   Korea Centers for Disease Control & Prevention, "Trend of current smoking rates among Korean adults aged 19 and over, 2007-2017," *Public Health Weekly Report*, 23-May-2019. [Online]. Available: http://www.cdc.go.kr/board.es?mid=a30501000000&bid=0031&list_no=143996&act=view. [Accessed: 25-Sep-2019].

» Discussion

While the results section of an experiment report presents data and statistical analysis, the discussion presents the authors' interpretation of this data. In other words, the discussion finds meaning in the data. It is typical only to discuss main trends or patterns, not to mention every data point here. The discussion can be an opportunity to compare results with other studies' findings, and to comment on whether findings were as expected or otherwise.

Activity 1

Review the example, 'The Effect of a Diamond Cubic Polypropylene Straw Structure on Protecting Duck Eggs from Impact.'

1. What main finding is explained here?

_____

_____

2. What comparison is made with other studies?

_____

_____

Activity 2

Consider the population pyramid shown in Fig. 1. Explain the general patterns or trends, suggesting possible causes and/ or effects.

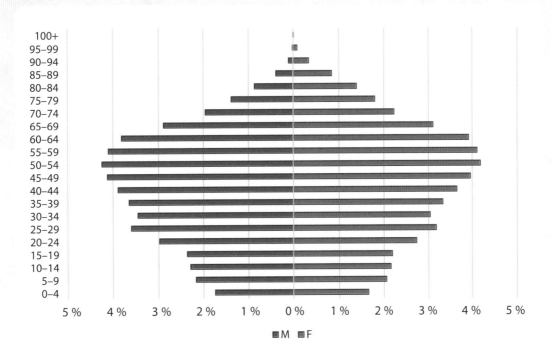

Fig. 1. 2022 South Korean population pyramid [1]

_____

_____

_____

_____

Reference

[1] "Population Pyramids of the World from 1950 to 2100: Republic of Korea 2022," *populationpyramid.net*, Jun. 21, 2022. https://www.populationpyramid.net/republic-of-korea/2022/ (accessed Jun. 21, 2022).

» Conclusion

The conclusion summarizes the other sections of the report. It gathers information from each section to reinforce the objectives and aim of the experiment. The author:

- restates the objectives of the experiment,
- reviews the main results and findings,
- states implications, e.g., for policy,
- recommends future research, and
- may pose final thoughts.

Activity 1

Review "The Effect of a Diamond Cubic Polypropylene Straw Structure on Protecting Duck Eggs from Impact" (pp. 52–55).

1. Underline the restatement of the objective.

2. What final thoughts do the authors leave for the readers?

_____

_____

Activity 2

Write a conclusion that summarizes the objectives and results, and add your own final thoughts. The key results from a study on the impact of the increase in cigarette taxes are presented below.

Objective:

• The purpose of this study is to estimate the financial and social effects of the price increase of cigarettes in Korea from 4,500 to 10,000 won.

Key Results:

• Korean families of low- and middle-income households bear the greatest impact.
• Both urban and rural Korean families are sensitive to higher price fluctuations.

Conclusion:

_____

_____

_____

_____

_____

_____

_____

_____

_____

_____

_____

_____

_____

_____

» References

The references section shows the reader how to find all of the published sources that are cited in the experiment report. Since many reports are similar, or replicate a study, it is important to give credit to the researchers who have prepared the foundation for your research. List the relevant references that you have cited in your report here.

Many technical reports use the Institute of Electrical and Electronics Engineers (IEEE) style, but each discipline uses its own style. References may vary based on discipline and publication form (e.g., website, book, journal).

The main components of a reference usually include:
- authors' names
- title of the article, patent, conference paper, etc.
- title of journal or book
- page numbers, year of publication, access date.

Signpost See the Research Skills section (page 158) to learn how to reference your sources in more detail.

Styles of Writing

While there are very general levels of writing complexity (sentences, paragraphs, reports), there are also specific styles or genres of writing that are used in different contexts. After learning the basics of sentences, paragraphs, and reports, this section will help writers to refine their skills, and tailor their writing to particular situations. Subsections of this chapter cover styles of writing, give examples, and help learners to understand how to improve their writing through various activities.

This section covers:

- Scientific Writing
- Definitions
- Processes
- Comparing and Contrasting
- Cause and Effect

1 Scientific Writing

Scientific writing is defined as scientists' technical writing, written for other scientists to read. *Science writing*, on the other hand, is writing for a general audience about scientific topics [1]. In this textbook we are concerned with *scientific* writing. In scientific writing it is important to be clear and concise, so it is best to avoid descriptive, wordy language. Writing should be impersonal, so the passive voice (e.g., "Chemical A was added to Chemical B.") is common in scientific writing.

Reference

[1]   N. Sheffield, "Science writing vs. scientific writing," *Scientific writing resource*, 2013. [Online]. Available: https://cgi.duke.edu/web/sciwriting/index.php?action=science_writing. [Accessed: 18-May-2019].

» Hedging

'Hedging your bets' is a gambling term meaning the avoidance of risking too much on one single outcome. Put simply, if you do not hedge your bets, you are more likely to lose. In academic written English, it is similarly important not to risk too much with a definitive statement that could be proven false.

Instead of the absolute or definitive statement "X causes Y," we should use "X may cause Y" or "X is likely to cause Y."

Hedging strategies allow the writer to make claims based on research while allowing for other points of view which may be contrary, and even more valid. Such strategies are common in academic writing because in most disciplines new evidence is continually found, so it is impossible to make absolute or definitive statements.

There are three common ways that researchers use hedging in their writing: reporting verbs, adverbs, and modal verbs.

Reporting Verbs

Indicate	Propose	Assume	Estimate
Suggest	Appear	Tend to	Argue

Definitive Statement:

Red meat, particularly processed red meat, causes cancer.

Hedged Statement:

Red meat, particularly processed red meat, *appears* to cause cancer.

Adverbs

Often	Almost	Occasionally	Sometimes
Quite	Usually	Probably	Possibly	Likely

Definitive Statement:

A diet that is high in animal protein *is* not as healthy as a diet that is high in plant protein

Hedged Statement:

A diet that is high in animal protein *is likely* not as healthy as a diet that is high in plant protein.

Modal Verbs

Strength of claim	Modal verb
Strong	Will/would
	Must
	Should
	Can/could
Weak	May

Definitive Statement:

The most recent research shows that the Mediterranean diet *is* the healthiest diet in the world.

Hedged Statement:

The most recent research shows that the Mediterranean diet *may* be the healthiest diet in the world.

» Being Concise

"If it is possible to cut a word out, always cut it out." [1]

In scientific writing it is important to be clear and concise. Avoid unnecessary words, and make your points efficiently and clearly. Using more words than necessary is known as 'wordiness.' Descriptive, wordy language is more time-consuming—and therefore frustrating—to read.

Reference

[1]   G. Orwell, "Politics and the English language," *Horizon: A review of literature and art*, vol. 13, no. 76, London, pp. 252–265, 1946.

Examples

1. The current paper is going to describe the commonly enjoyed hobby of collecting old comic books. (16 words)
   Collecting old comic books is enjoyable. (6 words)
2. The experiment revealed that when salt water is placed in a container with fresh water, the salt water will sink because salt water is denser than fresh water. (28 words)
   Salt water sinks below fresh water because salt water is denser. (11 words)
3. In many people's opinion, artificial intelligence will change and improve our lives for the better in the future. (18 words)
   Many people believe that artificial intelligence will improve people's lives. (10 words)

Activity 1

Match the wordy form with the short form in the table below. Write the letters in the middle column.

Wordy form			Short form	
1	Ask a question	1 =	A	Because/ Since
2	At the present time	2 =	B	While
3	In the event that	3 =	C	Ask
4	In the near future	4 =	D	Same
5	Due to the fact that	5 =	E	Commute
6	For the reason that	6 =	F	Many
7	In light of the fact that	7 =	G	Each
8	Is able to	8 =	H	A few
9	Each and every	9 =	I	Soon
10	Exact same	10 =	J	Always
11	In every instance	11 =	K	Because/ Since
12	In this day and age	12 =	L	Last/finally
13	During the time that	13 =	M	Yellow
14	Last, but not least	14 =	N	Return
15	First and foremost	15 =	O	Small
16	A large number of	16 =	P	Can
17	Few in number	17 =	Q	Now
18	Small in size	18 =	R	Postponed
19	Yellow in color	19 =	S	Because/ Since
20	Six in number	20 =	T	If
21	Return back	21 =	U	Six
22	Good benefit	22 =	V	Today/nowadays/these days
23	Commute back and forth	23 =	W	Benefit
24	Postponed until later	24 =	X	First

Activity 2

Rewrite the following paragraphs so that they are less wordy, and easier to read. Use 50 words or fewer.

You should place the instrument on a flat work surface capable of safely supporting the weight of the instrument. The instrument is about 5.7 kg in weight. If there is excessive vibration during readings, this has a tendency to cause poor repeatability, so a secure work surface is needed. At least a minimum of 8 cm clearance around the whole instrument is required to make sure the ventilation is completely optimal. (71 words)

_____

_____

_____

_____

The number of fuses is two, and both are located internally in the instrument. First, Fuse Number 1 is located on the main printed circuit board near the power connector. Second, Fuse Number 2 is located on the power supply. In the event that there is a fuse failure, which is a very rare occurrence, this may indicate malfunction of the equipment, and service by qualified personnel is highly preferable. (70 words)

_____

_____

_____

_____

» Parallel Structures

Another obstruction to clarity is use of nonparallel structures. A series of ideas or phrases should have parallel grammatical structure. In other words, the phrases or clauses in the list should be structured similarly. By balancing the items in a series so that they have the same kind of structure, the sentences will be clearer, and easier to read.

Examples

Nonparallel Structure

The experiment has a number of major flaws: researchers failed to account for the Magnus Effect, did not calculate air resistance correctly, and the testing equipment was not calibrated properly.

Parallel Structure

The experiment has a number of major flaws: researchers failed to account for the Magnus effect, did not calculate air resistance correctly, and did not calibrate the testing equipment properly.

With Coordinating Conjunctions

Coordinating conjunctions (*for*, *and*, *nor*, *but*, *or*, *yet*, *so*) join independent clauses. However, when these clauses (including reduced clauses) do not match in structure, the sentence is unbalanced and nonparallel.

Nonparallel

When conducting an experiment, it is important that all of the equipment is in good working order, and to clean it before starting.

Parallel

When conducting an experiment, it is important that all of the equipment is in good working order, and that it is clean before starting.

With Correlative Conjunctions

Correlative conjunctions, such as those below, join clauses together in a specific manner. The clauses must be parallel for the sentence to be grammatical. Otherwise this confuses the reader.

- Either A or B
- Neither A nor B
- Both A and B
- Not only A but also B
- Whether A or B

Nonparallel

Global warming is caused not only by deforestation, but also people burn fossil fuels.

Parallel

Global warming is caused not only by deforestation, but also by the burning of fossil fuels.

With Comparative Phrases or Clauses

When joining two clauses or phrases to make comparisons, words such as *than, as, as well as,* are commonly used.

Nonparallel

To eat nutritious meals is as beneficial to your health as exercising regularly.

Parallel

Eating nutritious meals is as beneficial to your health as exercising regularly.

Activity 1

Read the following sentences and correct any that does not use parallel structure.

1. He picked up a thermometer, a note pad, and began recording the temperatures.

_____

_____

_____

2. Most people responded that they would rather type on a laptop computer than to type on a tablet computer.

_____

_____

_____

3. The website is popular among users because it is fast, convenient, and has hourly updates.

_____

_____

_____

4. Nobody could dissuade the participants from speaking with the press, nor keep them from revealing the results.

_____

_____

_____

5. When examining the effects of stress on the body it is common to discuss three biological responses: the hormonal response, and the cardiovascular response, and the immune response.

_____

_____

_____

» Other Aspects of Scientific Writing

Do not use the following writing techniques when writing academic or formal assignments.

Problem	Correction
Coordinating Conjunctions • Replace with transitions at the beginning of a sentence	~~So this method is effective~~. Thus, this method is effective.
Abbreviations	~~TV~~ – television
Acronyms and initialisms • Do not use an acronym unless you first write out the full term and put the acronym in brackets	Post – Traumatic Stress Disorder (PTSD)
Truncations	~~Sat.~~ – Saturday
Contractions	~~Won't~~ – Will not ~~They're~~ – They are
Slang/Informal Language Texting ***Emoticons should never be used***	~~Wanna~~ – Want to ~~C u soon~~ – See you soon *^^*
Singular Nouns • Replace with plural nouns when talking about things in general	~~An apple is crunchier than an orange~~. Apples are crunchier than oranges.
Gender-exclusive Language • Do not use pronouns, terms, or expressions which exclude a gender	~~Mankind~~ – Humankind ~~Fireman~~ - Firefighter ~~If a child misbehaves, he should be punished~~. If children misbehave, they should be punished.
Etc./and so on/…	~~Carrots, cucumbers, etc. have many vitamins~~. Vegetables such as carrots or cucumbers have many vitamins.
Terms that are not understood internationally	~~I have a promise tonight~~. I have plans/an appointment tonight.
Digits • Do not use digits for numbers nine and under, rounded numbers, or numbers at the beginning of sentences (with the exception of dates)	~~There were 8 students in class~~. There were eight students in class.

💡 Tip

You should use digits if you are using integers greater than nine, percentages, dates, eras, fractions, money, decimals, surveys, scores, or other types of specific numbers.

Activity 1

Rewrite the following sentences to correct the inappropriate academic language.

1. SKKU was the first uni in Korea when it opened in thirteen ninety eight. At first, SKKU focused on teaching material related only to Confucianism, but now students can study film, Russian, engineering, etc.

_____

_____

_____

2. Seon Ah's doggie died in Feb. after being pretty sick for a looooong time. ㅜㅜ

_____

_____

_____

3. On Thurs. a policeman is needed to man the gate at the festival because there's gonna be people who think it's okay to bring alcohol into a children's event.

_____

_____

_____

4. Dae Hui's aircon had been broken for 5 days in 38 degree weather. But he couldn't call a repair guy to fix it because his handphone was also broken.

_____

_____

5. If a student is late for the quiz, test, exam, and so on, he will not be allowed extra time to complete it. And he will also lose participation marks cause he was not in class for the full time.

_____

_____

Using Certain Pronouns

When writing high level academic papers, it is sometimes appropriate for advanced students to use personal pronouns; however, when learning how to write, students should try to avoid:

I/Me/My/Mine	Direct personal opinion should be replaced with research or logical arguments.	~~I think this cancer drug is effective.~~ Research shows this cancer drug is effective.
You/Your/Yours	In some cases, using 'you' may be inappropriate or offensive to the audience.	~~You should not get divorced.~~ People should not get divorced.
We/Our/Ours	Academic writing should be used to communicate to a wide audience not just to your particular group.	~~In our culture, we eat *kimchi*.~~ In Korea, the locals eat kimchi.
I/We vs. You Us vs. Them	Try to avoid language which unnecessarily polarizes groups.	~~We have different views than those people.~~ Students have different views than teachers.

Writers should also avoid asking simple questions or posing questions directly to their readers.

Asking the reader a direct question. • The reader cannot respond to your question while reading. In addition, it is the responsibility of the writer to give information to the reader.	Why do you think junk food is harmful?
Answering a simple question immediately. • Concise writing is better in short assignments. Additionally, it is better to prove your argument with evidence	Is junk food unhealthy? Yes, junk food is unhealthy.
Giving an answer as an incomplete sentence. • Sentence fragments should not occur in academic writing	Is junk food unhealthy? Yes.

The questions given above could be rephrased as the following statements:

Give your reader answers instead of posing new questions.	~~Why do you think junk food is harmful?~~ Junk food is harmful because it contains an excess of calories and fat.
State your position clearly in one sentence where possible.	~~Is junk food unhealthy? Yes, junk food is unhealthy.~~ ~~Is junk food unhealthy? Yes.~~ Junk food is unhealthy for a number of reasons. Junk food is unhealthy because it contributes to heart disease and diabetes.

Definitions

Most technical writing uses vocabulary which is uncommon in everyday language. Readers often need such terms to be explained with a definition, which may range in length from a word to a paragraph. Definitions commonly use synonyms, class, negation, and examples.

Synonyms

Synonyms are words or phrases with similar meanings. For example, an *integer* is a *whole number*, and *Passer montanus* is the *Eurasian tree sparrow*. A thesaurus can be useful to find synonyms; however, it is important to be cautious. For example, the word *spectrum* has 52 synonyms in three popular thesauruses [1], [2], [3]:

ambit, array, assortment, catalog, choice, chromatic spectrum, collection, colors, compass, continuum, cross section, distribution, diversity, extent, farrago, field, gamut, hotchpotch, hue cycle, intermixture, jumble, line-up, lot, medley, mélange, miscellany, mishmash, mix, mixed bag, mixture, motley collection, multiplicity, orbit, pick 'n' mix, potpourri, prism, purview, rainbow, range, ranges, repertoire, salmagundi, scale, scope, selection, sequence, series, span, sphere, sweep, variegation, variety

Some of these words are clearly very different, e.g., *choice* and *rainbow*, while others—e.g., *jumble*, *line-up*, *mishmash*, *motley collection*—are likely inappropriate in a scientific writing genre. It is therefore important after selecting a candidate synonym, to find synonyms for *that*. If the synonym's synonyms differ greatly from the original term, it is probably inappropriate.

After selecting an appropriate synonym, this can be included in an explanatory sentence. For example:
- The *electromagnetic spectrum* is the full range of wavelengths of electromagnetic radiation.

Note that *spectrum* is defined as *range* here.

References
[1]   S. Hawker and M. Waite, Eds., *Concise Oxford thesaurus*, 3rd ed. Oxford: Oxford University Press, 2007.
[2]   G. Breslin and L. Gilmour, Eds., *Collins English thesaurus*, 5th ed. Glasgow: HarperCollins, 2013.
[3]   B. A. Kipfer, Ed., *Roget's 21st century thesaurus*, 3rd ed. New York: Dell, 2013.

Activity 1

Write a list of appropriate synonyms for *acute* (as in *acute angle* [an angle less than 90°]), and another list for *acute* (as in *acute disease* [a short-term illness]).

Angle: _____

_____

Disease: _____

_____

Classification

It is often useful to explain that something is a member of a larger class. This helps the reader to situate it. For example:

The *Eurasian tree sparrow* is a small, common songbird species in the *Passeridae* family.

The readers will likely understand what a *songbird* is, and this may sufficiently satisfy their curiosity. Those who wish to learn more can easily find out what *Passeridae* means.

Activity 2

Write a sentence similar to the example above, for the term *methane*.

_____

_____

Sometimes a sentence is insufficient to explain levels of categories, so a paragraph may be required.

Example

Fats

Fats are classified as cis-unsaturated, saturated, and trans fats, and each type affects the human body differently. Cis-unsaturated fats are typically liquid. They have double bonds in their fatty acid chains, so they contain fewer hydrogen atoms than saturated fats do. Therefore, since people obtain energy from fats by oxidizing the carbon-hydrogen bond, these fats have fewer calories than saturated fats have. Saturated fats, meanwhile, have no double bonds, so they are more uniform, and they pack together more tightly, forming a more rigid structure. As a result, they form deposits in arteries, causing vascular problems for many people. Finally, trans fats are unsaturated fats in which the arrangement of the double bonds forms a straighter molecule than that in the normal cis configuration. It is widely understood that human lipase can only process cis-configured unsaturated fatty acids, so trans fats tend not to break down easily, and therefore cause serious health concerns. It is therefore important to understand the names of these types of fat when choosing a healthy and balanced diet.

Negation

While it is important to inform the reader of what something *is*, it is also important to explain what it *isn't*. For example:

- Eurasian tree sparrows are not to be confused with American tree sparrows, which are in the *Passerellidae* family.
- A *horse* is a large mammal in the *Equidae* family, but it is not a zebra.
  (Zebras are also members of this family.)

This sets definitions' bounds or limits.

Activity 3

Write a sentence explaining what rust [$Fe_2O_3 \cdot nH_2O$, $FeO(OH)$, and $Fe(OH)_3$] isn't. In other words, explain what is *not* classified as rust. To do this, you may also have to explain briefly what rust *is*.

_____

_____

Examples

People are often good at extrapolating definitions from examples. For example, read the following sentence.

> A *mubb* is a category of mammal including tigers, lions, leopards, and cheetahs.

Mubb clearly means *big cat*. In fact, there is no English word *mubb*; this syllable simply follows English pronunciation rules well, so it sounds like an English word [1]. Nevertheless, even though the word *mubb* does not exist, the reader can understand it because the common feature of tigers, lions, leopards, and cheetahs is clear.

Reference

[1]   M. S. Vitevitch, P. A. Luce, J. Charles-Luce, and D. Kemmerer, "Phonotactics and Syllable Stress: Implications for the Processing of Spoken Nonsense Words," *Lang. Speech*, vol. 40, no. 1, pp. 47–62, 1997.

Activity 4

Think of something that has a few examples. Change its name to *mubb*, and write a sentence listing some examples like the sentence above. Read it to another student, who should guess what *mubb* means.

_____

_____

Definition Paragraphs

Depending on the intended audience, some definitions only need a short explanation with a synonym or a few examples. However, some readers need more details, and a full paragraph may be required.

Example

Number Theory

Number theory is the field of pure mathematics usually concerning the properties of integers. For example, number theory proves that an integer is divisible by three if and only if the sum of its digits is also divisible by three. Such proofs have historically interested many scholars, largely because several apparently elementary theories remain unproven. For example, Goldbach's Conjecture [1] states that all even numbers greater than two can be expressed as the sum of two prime numbers. This appears true, but no researcher has yet proven it. Another classic unproven theory, the Ulam Spiral, claims that when integers are arranged spirally, and all non-prime numbers are then removed, the remaining numbers form diagonal lines [2]. The elusive nature of proofs to such apparently simple concepts has fascinated mathematicians from the ancient Greeks to contemporary researchers so much that Gauss claimed that "[m]athematics is the queen of the sciences—and number theory is the queen of mathematics" [3]. The mysterious nature of apparently simple integers has thus given number theory enduring appeal.

References

[1]   C. Goldbach, "Lettre XLIII [Letter 43]." 07-Jun-1742.

[2]   M. L. Stein, S. M. Ulam, and M. B. Wells, "A visual display of some properties of the distribution of primes," *Am. Math. Mon.*, vol. 71, no. 5, pp. 516–520, May 1964.

[3]   W. S. von Waltershausen, *Gauss: Zum gedächtnis [Gauss: In memory]*. Leipzig: S. Hirzel, 1856.

Activity 5

Choose a term from this list, and write a short paragraph to define it. Try to include synonyms, class, negation, and/or examples (in the order of your choice).

Amphibian	Covalent bond	Triple point	Semiconductor

_____

_____

_____

_____

_____

_____

_____

_____

_____

_____

_____

_____

_____

3 Processes

Scientists often have to explain processes. Processes are procedures: they have a fixed sequence of steps. For example, butterflies begin life in eggs, then caterpillars emerge from the eggs. The caterpillars become pupae, and they finally *metamorphose* (literally *change shape*) into butterflies. It is impossible to change the order of these steps. Some processes are cycles, e.g., the water cycle, so these do not have a fixed start and end, but the steps nevertheless occur in a fixed order.

The examples above are processes that explain how something works. Sometimes we have to give instructions *to do* something, for example how to make copper(II) sulfate [$CuSO_4(H_2O)_x$] crystals. This may seem similar to a recipe in a cookbook, e.g., how to bake a cake, but scientific writing has a different style. Recipes often use imperative syntax (the grammar for instructions), e.g., "heat the oil", "add the herbs", and "stir continuously." Note the verb forms here: *heat*, *add*, and *stir*. These are commands, and they are uncommon in scientific writing. Scientific processes often explain what you did in an experiment so the reader can replicate it. It may be tempting to say "I boiled 100 mL of water. Then I added 50 g of sodium citrate." However, this can seem childish. The reader already knows that you did it, and it feels more modest to remove the agent (you) from the explanation. The passive voice is therefore used more in scientific writing, e.g., "100 mL of water *was boiled*. Then 50 g of sodium citrate *was added*."

Example Experiment Method

Copper(II) sulfate pentahydrate [$CuSO_4(H_2O)_5$] crystals were made by the following process. First 20 mL of diluted sulfuric acid [$H_2SO_4(aq)$ 0.5M] was poured into an Erlenmeyer flask, and heated in water. Copper(II) oxide (CuO) powder was added to the flask by spatula, and the mixture was stirred with a glass rod. Copper(II) oxide was added continually (approx. 1 g in total) until it would no longer dissolve. The mixture was then filtered to remove excess copper(II) oxide powder, and the resulting filtrate was heated until the volume was halved. The remaining solution was poured onto a watch glass, and left at room temperature for one week, during which the remaining liquid evaporated. Through this process, copper(II) sulfate pentahydrate crystals were deposited on the watch glass.

Example Explanation of How Something Happens

Four-stroke internal combustion engines—typical car engines—change chemical energy to kinetic energy by combusting fuel. First, the downward motion of the piston sucks in fuel and air through the intake valve. The valve closes, and the fuel-air mixture is compressed by the piston's return motion. The spark plug then ignites the fuel with an electrical discharge, and the expansion of the fuel resulting from its combustion pushes the piston down again. It is this motion that turns the crankshaft, and in a vehicle this eventually turns the wheels. The combusted fuel is expelled through the exhaust valve by the piston's final upward return (the fourth stroke), this valve then closes, and the process repeats. In this way, internal combustion engines convert the chemical energy stored in fuel to kinetic energy, powering the machine.

Note that this contains more active verbs than in explanations of experiment methods.

Activity 1

1. Identify the controlling idea in the paragraph about internal combustion engines.
2. How many main stages are in the process?
3. Draw a diagram of the engine's process in this box.

Activity 2

Consider a simple experiment that you have done recently. Explain the process in a paragraph.

_____

_____

_____

_____

_____

_____

_____

_____

_____

_____

_____

_____

_____

_____

_____

4 Comparing and Contrasting

Compare and contrast writing takes two or more topics and examines their similarities, differences, or similarities and differences. Unlike persuasive writing, compare and contrast writing does not make a judgement or take a particular stance on how one topic is better or worse than the other. Rather, this type of writing looks at the topics objectively. However, even though you will be comparing or contrasting two or more different topics, you need to make sure that you still have one thesis statement. In addition, you should also give an approximately equal amount of space to both topics to ensure a balanced assignment.

Compare and contrast writing is often used in academic writing to objectively examine multiple topics or options. For example, students might look at two dynasties in a history class, different products in a business paper, or more than one styles of dance in a performing arts program. Nevertheless, employees may also use compare and contrast writing in a non-academic context in order to compare two different financial packages available at a bank or credit card company, explore two travel options for a tourist agency, or various course choices at a university.

In this section you will:

- Learn different kinds of compare and contrast structure
- Examine a compare and contrast essay
- Learn to identify good and bad topic combinations
- Practice Venn and T-Chart brainstorming
- Use compare and contrast connecting words
- Write your own compare and contrast assignment using the skills learned in this section

Activity 1

Answer the following questions about holidays.

1. What is your favorite holiday? What do you like most about this holiday?

2. How do you think traditional holidays like Chuseok and Seollal will change in fifty years?

Thanksgiving and Chuseok: Unique Festivals for Unique Cultures

At Thanksgiving in the United States (U.S.), and Chuseok in Korea, families gather for an autumn feast in celebration of the harvest. Though these holidays share clear similarities, they are unique in their own ways. Firstly, they differ in origin. Thanksgiving is a continuation of the traditional British harvest festival, and records show that a particularly good harvest festival was celebrated in 1621 in Plymouth (now in Massachusetts). Chuseok, meanwhile, dates to the Silla Dynasty, possibly originating as a weaving festival, and possibly as a celebration of victory over Balhae. The agricultural meaning associated with the festival today was ascribed only later. Today, Americans celebrate Thanksgiving with relatives to give thanks for many aspects of life, with a focus on the present. Chuseok, however, also involves remembrance of the past through ancestral rites, largely due to Shaman and Confucian traditions. Finally, both holidays involve events outside family celebrations. U.S. students often act in plays idealizing early Thanksgiving feasts shared with Native Americans, and many people watch American football games. In Korea, some people watch traditional sports such as archery and *ssireum* (traditional Korean wrestling). These two holidays thus differ from one another in distinct ways, yet they share a similar focus: a celebration of the harvest.

Activity 2

Answer the following questions about the essay you have just read.

1. Does this paragraph focus more on the similarities or the differences between the two holidays?

2. Make a list of the similarities and differences between two other holidays.

Structure

There are three basic structures found in compare and contrast writing: focus on the similarities, focus on the difference, and focus on the similarities and differences. The following structural examples are based on comparing and contrasting North American and Korean Christmas.

Focus on the Similarities

Support	Topic	Korean and North American Information
Point 1	Food	Eaten with loved ones, special dessert
Point 2	Symbols	Christmas tree, red and green, lights
Point 3	Santa	Santa: large man who wears red, beard, delivers gifts

Focus on the Differences

Support	Topic	Korean Information	North American Information
Point 1	Food	Who: eaten with romantic partner or friends at a restaurant What: pizza, steak, wine, purchased Christmas cake	Who: eaten with family at home What: homemade turkey, ham, or goose, Christmas cookies, traditional dried fruit cake
Point 2	Decorations	Mostly public: shopping areas, major streets, city areas Home: perhaps a small tree	Equally public and private: elaborate indoor and outdoor displays in homes, businesses, and public places
Point 3	Santa	1 reindeer (Rudolph), unknown home, family, and life	Several (perhaps 9) reindeer, Santa lives at the North Pole with his wife (Mrs. Claus) and elves (who make the toys)

Focus on the Similarities and Differences

Support	Topic	Similarities	Differences
Point 1	Food	Eaten with loved ones, special desserts	Korea: romantic partner/friends at restaurant eating pizza, steak, wine North America: family at home, homemade turkey, ham, or goose, Christmas cookies, traditional fruit cake
Point 2	Decorations	Christmas tree, red and green, lights	Korea: mostly public, perhaps a small tree at home North America: elaborate indoor and outdoor displays in homes, businesses, and public areas
Point 3	Santa	Santa – large man who wears red, beard, delivers gifts	Korea: 1 reindeer, Santa's life unknown North America: 9 reindeer, North Pole, wife, helpers

Topic Selection

When choosing your topics for a compare and contrast assignment, you need to make sure that the topics are neither too similar nor too different. For instance, hamburgers and cheeseburgers are too similar to each other with the exception of a slice of cheese. In contrast, while ice cream and Siberia are both cold, the similarities end there. While deciding what you are going to write about, you should find two topics that are part of the same category with enough differences to make your paper interesting.

Activity 3

Look at the following topics and mark if they are too similar (S), too different (D), or good topics for a compare and contrast paragraph (G).

1. *Kimbap* vs. sandwiches
2. Japan vs. Japan Airlines (JAL)
3. Scuba diving vs. space walking
4. Caffe latte vs. Americano
5. Action movie vs. Korean drama

6. Seollal vs. Solar New Year's Day
7. Turtles vs. snails
8. *Gochujang* vs. *jjimjilbang*
9. Seoul vs. Gyeongju
10. Vampires vs. witches

Venn Diagram Brainstorming

There are two ways to brainstorm for compare and contrast assignments. The first way is a Venn diagram, which is a visual way to show the similarities and differences between two topics. The following Venn Diagram shows the similarities and differences between Thanksgiving in the United States and Chuseok in South Korea.

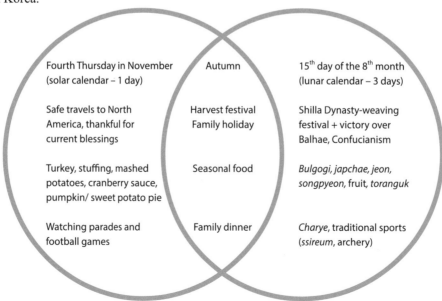

Fourth Thursday in November (solar calendar – 1 day)

Autumn

15th day of the 8th month (lunar calendar – 3 days)

Safe travels to North America, thankful for current blessings

Harvest festival
Family holiday

Shilla Dynasty-weaving festival + victory over Balhae, Confucianism

Turkey, stuffing, mashed potatoes, cranberry sauce, pumpkin/ sweet potato pie

Seasonal food

Bulgogi, japchae, jeon, songpyeon, fruit, *toranguk*

Watching parades and football games

Family dinner

Charye, traditional sports (*ssireum,* archery)

T-Chart Brainstorming

The second way to brainstorm for a compare and contrast assignment is a T-chart. This method works better for longer and more complicated assignments because there is more space available to develop each point. In this type of brainstorming, write the category on the left side and brainstorm the similarities and differences for each topic in the other columns. To differentiate between similarities and differences, use different colors of highlighters or underline the points that are different.

Category	The United States: Thanksgiving	Korea: Chuseok
When	• 4th Thursday in November • Solar calendar • Public holiday: One day	• 15th day of the 8th month • Lunar calendar • Public holiday: Three-five days
Origin	• Spanish 16th century/British 17th century • European and Native American harvest festivals • Good harvest/safe travels to North America	• Shilla Dynasty • A feast after a weaving contest • Victory over Balhae kingdom
Current Focus	• Family holiday • Harvest festival • Being thankful for present blessings	• Family holiday • Harvest festival • Ancestral memorial rituals
Food	• Turkey • Stuffing, mashed potatoes, sweet potatoes, squash • Pumpkin or sweet potato pie	• *Bulgogi* • *Japchae, jeon, toranguk* • *Songpyeon*, fruit
Activities	• Family dinner • Parades • Football games	• Family dinner • *Charye* and cleaning ancestors' graves • Traditional sports: *ssireum*, archery, tug of war

Compare and Contrast Connecting Words

Throughout your compare and contrast assignment, you should use connecting words to connect ideas and to make smooth transitions between different sections. The following are examples of both types of words.

Compare (Similarities)

likewise	similarly	furthermore	in addition	additionally
as	in the same way	also	too	moreover

Contrast (Differences)

yet	however	alternatively	conversely	although
in contrast	on the other hand	on the contrary	but	nevertheless

Activity 4

Take one of the good topic combinations in Activity 3, and brainstorm the similarities and differences in your notebook using a Venn diagram.

Activity 5

Use the ideas you brainstormed in Activity 4, and link them with connecting words to make full sentences.

Signpost See pages 14–20, 35, and 39 for more information on connecting words. Some of the connecting words given above are coordinating conjunctions while others are subordinating conjunction words or transitions. Make sure you understand the differences between these kinds of words before you make your own sentences.

Activity 6

Use the sentences you made in Activity 5 to write a well-organized paragraph by adding a topic sentence and concluding sentence.

5 Cause and Effect

Cause and effect writing shows the relationship between two events when one results from the other. It is a common style found in academic reports. For example, engineers may investigate the failings of a weight-bearing structure in a collapsed building, or the effects of soil erosion, while pharmacists may consider the effects of particular chemicals on the human body. It is important to note that correlation between two events does not imply a causal relationship. For example, between 2000 and 2009, U.S. per capita consumption of cheese correlated with the number of people who died by becoming tangled in their bedsheets (r=0.947) [1]. Cause and effect writing thus requires critical thinking skills, and writers must analyze how events relate and connect to each other.

Reference
[1]   T. Vigen, *Spurious correlations*. New York: Hachette Books, 2015.

In this section you will:

- examine a model cause and effect paragraph
- analyze different methods and organizational patterns of cause and effect writing
- examine how cause and effect connectors are used to show a relationship
- write a cause and effect paragraph.

Activity 1

Answer the following questions about Cheonggyecheon.

1. Have you ever visited Cheonggyecheon? What are Cheonggyecheon's features?

_____

_____

_____

_____

_____

_____

_____

2. What do you think are some of the advantages or disadvantages of having a stream or river flowing through the center of a city?

_____

_____

_____

_____

_____

_____

_____

The Restoration of Cheonggyecheon

Between 2003 and 2005, under the supervision of Mayor Lee Myung-bak, 5.8 km of central Seoul's long-hidden stream, Cheonggyecheon, was uncovered and restored [1]. This has brought widespread benefits to the city, but has also caused several problems. Prior to this project, Cheonggyecheon was covered by a large elevated twin-level highway which arguably caused the degeneration of central Seoul [2]. Demolition of this highway has opened an urban green belt bringing greatly-needed space and cleaner air to the city center [1], [3]. The effects of this regeneration on tourism are noteworthy: visitors report their support and satisfaction from both natural and artificial features [4]. Nevertheless, the project has been criticized for being a reimagination rather than a true regeneration [1], e.g., for consuming great amounts of energy by pumping 120,000 tons of water each day from the Han River [2], and for appearing to be a political platform for the mayor's presidential bid [2]. Cheonggyecheon's restoration has thus not been without controversy, but has also had positive effects on central Seoul.

References

[1]   J. Y. Lee and C. D. Anderson, "The restored Cheonggyecheon and the quality of life in Seoul," *J. Urban Technol.*, vol. 20, no. 4, pp. 3–22, 2013.

[2]   M.-R. Cho, "The politics of urban nature restoration: The case of Cheonggyecheon restoration in Seoul, Korea," *Int. Dev. Plan. Rev.*, vol. 32, no. 2, pp. 145–165, 2010.

[3]   J.-H. Shin and I.-K. Lee, "Cheong Gye Cheon restoration in Seoul, Korea," *Proc. Inst. Civ. Eng. - Civ. Eng.*, vol. 159, no. 4, pp. 162–170, 2006.

[4]   Y.-K. Lee, C.-K. Lee, J. Choi, S.-M. Yoon, and R. J. Hart, "Tourism's role in urban regeneration: examining the impact of environmental cues on emotion, satisfaction, loyalty, and support for Seoul's revitalized Cheonggyecheon stream district," *J. Sustain. Tour.*, vol. 22, no. 5, pp. 726–749, 2014.

Activity 2

Answer the following questions about the paragraph.

1. Does this paragraph state the effects from the restoration of Cheonggyecheon, the causes for the restoration of Cheonggyecheon, or both?

2. What are the three main effects of the restoration of Cheonggyecheon? For each supporting idea, find three supporting examples stated in the essay.

B1 _____ |————————————————————
                          |————————————————————

B2 _____ |————————————————————
                          |————————————————————

B3 _____ |————————————————————
                          |————————————————————

3. In your town or city, choose a historic, famous, or interesting place, and write down any effects it may have on the citizens and the town/city itself.

_____

_____

_____

_____

_____

_____

Organization of a Cause-Effect Paragraph

Once a topic has been given or chosen, the way the paragraph will be organized should be decided. A writer may wish to examine the causes, effects, or both.

Focus on Causes Method

Using this method, the writer will discuss the causes for an event or condition and develop and discuss each cause. In the following example, the writer will discuss the factors that can cause heart disease to increase.

A person has a poor diet.	
A person smokes.	The risk of heart disease increases.
A person has a family history of high blood pressure.	

Focus on Effects Method

Using this method, the writer will discuss the effects of an event or condition and develop and discuss each effect. In the following example, the writer will discuss the effects resulting from a poor diet.

	They may gain weight.
People have a poor diet.	They may suffer from fatigue.
	They may develop Type II diabetes.

Activity 3

Fill in the tables with appropriate information to complete the cause-effect relationship.

Ji Su goes to the library every day.	
Ji Su studies hard on the weekends.	
Ji Su takes extra classes.	

A country hosts the Olympic Games.	

Focus on Causes and Effects Method (Chain Organization)

Using this method, the writer will discuss the both the causes and effects of an event or condition. The effect from the previous point will then become the cause in the following point. The causes and effects are therefore linked like a chain with each having an influence on the next. In the following example, the writer will discuss the links leading from a poor diet to an increase in the risk of heart disease.

How diet affects health

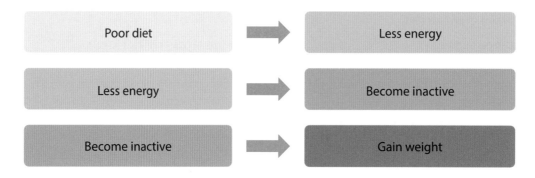

Getting a part time job

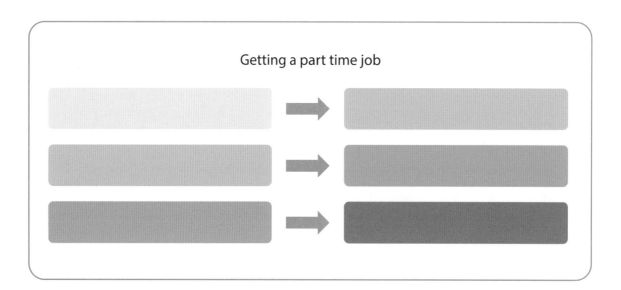

Cause-Effect Organization

When developing the causes or effects, you can organize the paragraph in two ways: order of importance and chronological (time) order.

1. Order of importance: This format is where ideas are arranged from the weakest to the strongest. In the paragraph on the restoration of Cheonggyecheon, the writer believes that the re-establishment of the cultural and historical heritage is the most important factor. A different writer, such as an economics or business major, may feel that the stimulation of the local economy is the most important and thereby the final effect to discuss.

2. Chronological order: This format is where ideas are arranged into a time order from what happened first to last. Cause-effect writing dealing with history is often arranged chronologically.

Cause-Effect Connecting Words

Just as connecting words are used in other types of writing, so too are they used to show or express the relationship between ideas.

Cause

Because Since As	the costs were high,	the project was canceled
As a result of As a consequence of Because of Due to	the high costs	

Effect

The costs were too high;	as a result, as a consequence, thus, therefore, consequently, hence,	the project was canceled

Activity 4

In the model paragraph, a number of connectors show cause/effect relationships. Read it again, and highlight any connectors.

Building Blocks

The basic foundation for all writing is the sentence. Grammatically sound sentences help writers to convey their message properly and accurately, but beyond grammar, there are also skills and techniques students can learn in order to enhance their writing and clarify their points. This section will help students to review basic grammar before moving into more complex skills and techniques students can use to improve their ability to write academically and objectively. A great deal of space is available for students to practice and perfect these skills before they try to bring them into longer paragraph and report assignments.

This section does not have to be followed linearly. Rather, the information covered in these subsections can be incorporated into various forms of writing and contexts. The main purpose of this section is to help students develop the skills necessary to enrich their sentences, and to improve their overall writing techniques.

This section covers:

- Articles
- Capitalization
- Prepositions
- Conditionals
- Modal auxiliary verbs
- Adjectives
- Active vs. Passive Voice
- Comparatives and Superlatives
- Using Non-English Words in English
- Paraphrasing and Summarizing
- Scientific Vocabulary and Collocations

1 Articles

"A" and "an" are indefinite articles used to identify general nouns while "the" is the definite article which is used to refer to specific nouns.

Examples:

Niels Bohr was **a** Danish physicist. (one of many Danish physicists)

Niels Bohr was **the** physicist who first drew the structure of the atom. (the first to do something)

The students found **an** empty classroom, so they could study. (any room is fine)

The students could not find **the** classroom for their English class. (the specific room)

Indefinite Articles

"A" is used with words that sound like consonants while "an" is used with words that sound like vowels. In some words, vowels sound like consonants, so they need an "a" while in some words, consonants sound like vowels and should be preceded by an "an."

Examples:

When she was **a** sophomore, Jeong Ah only spent **an** hour on **an** eight page essay about **a** United Nations agency, so her professor gave her **an** "F."

Countable and Uncountable Nouns

"A" and "an" can only be used with countable nouns.

Countable	Uncountable	Both
Pear	Rice	Do you want **a chocolate**? (individual piece) I do not like **chocolate**. (in general)
Dollar	Money	He does not have **a hair** on his head. (individual strand) She just dyed her **hair** red. (whole head of hair)
Horse	Love	Is there **an extra room** in International Hall? (classroom) Do you have **room** in your car for me? (space)
Pen	Information	Is there **a light** in each room? (light fixture) Our new house has more **light**. (natural light)
Table	Equipment	**A scary experience** happened today. (occurrence) I have enough **experience** for this job. (general)

Examples:

If you have a pen, I will write down information about equipment you can buy to make homemade chocolate.

» Definite Articles

Like many areas of English grammar, there are some exceptions in how definite articles are used. Nevertheless, "the" is usually used in the following situations:

Use	Examples
Something previously mentioned	There is an unoccupied chair, but the chair looks broken.
Something specific or unique	The professor for this class just arrived.
A group of people identified by an adjective or a population as a whole	the unemployed, the Spanish
Instruments	the piano
Superlatives	the fastest
Plural names of groups of people and places	the Kims, the Netherlands
Country names including 'republic' and 'united'	the Republic of Ireland, the United Kingdom
Buildings (unless the first word is the name of a place)	the Blue House
Oceans, seas, rivers, canals, gulfs, peninsulas, deserts	the Pacific Ocean, the Black Sea, the Amazon, the Panama Canal
Mountain, island, or lake groups	the Himalayas, the Canary Islands, the Connecticut Lakes
Geographical regions, points on the globe, location	the West, the Equator, Gwangju is in the southern part of Korea.

Do not use "the" in the following situations:

Use	Examples
Most languages, nationalities	English, Australian
Continents, most countries, states/provinces	Europe, Morocco, British Columbia
Buildings (if the first word is the name of a place)	Seoul Liberty Building
Cities/towns, streets	Incheon, Main Street
Bays, parks, individual mountains, islands, or lakes	James Bay, Hyde Park, Bukhan Mountain, Easter Island, Lake Louise
Directions (when comparing two places)	Nepal is north of India.

Grammar Tip

Using Non-English Words

Non-English words usually follow the same countable/uncountable rules.

Activity 1

Correct the articles in the following sentences.

1. Before going on a hike, remember to pack a water, the chocolate bars, and map.

2. Young children should learn the Korean before they learn second language.

3. At the pet shop beside the Summer Hill Park, there were a snakes, a iguana, and the turtle.

4. The Seoul is located on Korean Peninsula in South Korea, which is also called Republic of Korea.

5. Renee will not eat chicken because she has chicken for the pet.

6. Jenny had always wanted to work in the large company, but a company she wanted to work in would not hire her, so she joined small company instead.

7. White House is official residence for president of United States.

8. Homeless in Seoul often find shelter in a Seoul Station on cold nights.

9. Kennedys live on the St. Denis street which is located the north of St. Laurent street.

10. Chinese in the Taiwan speak Mandarin, and Chinese in Guangdong province speak Cantonese.

11. He wants to eat *kimchi*; however, *kimchi* in his refrigerator is now rotten.

12. June does not like the *ddeok*, but she ate piece of *ddeok* because it was served at her friend's wedding.

13. I would give you piece of paper, but there is no the paper left.

Activity 2

After reading the following passages, fill in the missing articles.

Yeon Hee has violin that costs over million dollars because she is professional violinist. She has been playing violin since she was three years old, and she won first prize in her second competition when she was only four. At age seven, she was accepted into prestigious Seoul Performing Arts Academy and quickly progressed to senior position in youth orchestra. Later, Yeon Hee moved to the London when she was 15 years old to pursue her dream of becoming professional violinist. These days Yeon Hee regularly plays with London Symphony Orchestra, but she has yet to be asked to be soloist.

Great Lakes are five lakes located along Canadian-American border. While each lake is a separate body of water, they are connected through rivers and canals. For instance, Niagara River connects Lake Huron to Lake Ontario at the city of Niagara Falls, and Welland Canal connects Lake Erie and Lake Ontario. Saint Lawrence River takes the water from all of these lakes to Atlantic Ocean by way of Quebec and Gaspé Peninsula. Water in these lakes provides water and power to many important North American cities surrounding lakes including Chicago, Detroit, and Toronto.

2 Capitalization

When English letters are written in their uppercase form, the process is called "capitalization." The following chart shows when letters are usually capitalized.

Use	Examples
The first word of a sentence	Exchange programs provide students with many benefits.
"I"	When I was in high school, I studied until midnight every night.
Every word in a title (except articles, prepositions with four or more letters, and coordinating conjunctions unless they appear at the beginning of a title)	*The Wind in the Willows*
Proper nouns (Specific or unique nouns)	
• Organizations	• the World Health Organization.
• Places	• Sungkyunkwan University is an old university.
• Brands	• Starbucks Coffee Company has built its reputation steadily over many years.
• Geographical regions	• There are many conflicts in the Middle East.
• Names, titles, names before titles, titles before names	• Professor Lee is a famous professor. • Aunt Sarah is my favorite aunt.
• Days, months, holidays	• In 2011, Children's Day, which is always on May 5th, fell on a Thursday.
Words such as adjectives, and languages that are derived from proper nouns	Spanish is spoken in Spain by Spaniards.
Course titles	Because he was a biology major, he took Introduction to Biology.

ⓥ Grammar Tip

Capitalization and Names

Some names have unique capitalization rules because of their origin.

Jane McNeil   Charles de Gaulle   Vincent van Gogh

Korean names are generally capitalized in one of four ways.

Young Sang Lee, Young-Sang Lee, Youngsang Lee, Lee Youngsang

Some people choose to write their given name as Yeongsang, which conforms to the South Korean government's standard system.

Activity 1

Read the following sentences, and highlight the words which should be capitalized.

1. before i went to portugal last year, i studied portuguese.

2. sam failed history 101 last year because history is his worst subject.

3. professor lee asked john whether he had finished reading jane austen's *pride and prejudice*.

4. there used to be a mr. pizza restaurant located very close to hyehwa station.

5. when korean thanksgiving falls on a monday, tuesday, or thursday, it is a five-day holiday, when it is a friday, saturday, or sunday, it is a four-day holiday, and when it is a wednesday, it is a three-day holiday.

6. there are many ways to experience nature in seoul: bukhan mountain, the han river, and the cheonggye stream.

7. after watching the movie *the devil wears prada*, jenny decided to go to new york city instead of visiting europe.

8. there is about 1,050 mg of sodium in a serving of shin ramyun which is surprisingly more sodium than the 1,010 mg found in a mcdonald's big mac.

9. lee hyo ri's song "chitty chitty bang bang" has nothing to do with ian fleming's 1964 novel by the same name.

10. professor webster is a south african anthropologist who is best known for his contribution to the anti-apartheid movement.

Activity 2

Read the following passages and highlight the letters which should be capitalized.

shanghai, in the people's republic of china, is a fabulous city to visit. tourists who love sports can visit during the chinese grand prix or watch the city's basketball team, the shanghai sharks play. for those who prefer to spend their time in museums, the shanghai art museum in people's square houses a large number of exhibitions. at night, the bund is a fantastic area to see historic buildings and view architecturally interesting buildings such as the oriental pearl tower across the huangpu river. therefore, there are many diverse places to visit and sites to see in shanghai.

ban ki-moon has had an interesting life. he was born in a small village in north chungcheong province, but in 1962, he won a red cross essay contest which allowed him to move to san francisco where he was able to improve his english skills. during his time in the united states of america, he met president john f. kennedy. after attending seoul national university and harvard university, he became a diplomat and later, the head of the ministry of foreign affairs and trade in south korea. he presently holds the position of secretary general at the united nations. thus, his life is an inspiration for younger koreans who want to serve their country on an international level.

3

Prepositions

» Prepositions of Time

The following prepositions are commonly used to discuss time.

Preposition	Use	Examples
At	Precise times	Class begins at 9 a.m. We take a break at dinnertime.
In	General times • months, years, centuries, long periods	He was born in July in 1980. Sungkyunkwan University was founded in the 14th century. We have class in the morning.
On	Specific times • dates and days	His birthday is on July 31. On White Day, men give women candy.
During	Development through a period	During the month of July, there is often a lot of rain. During the Seollal period, there are no classes.
For	Length of time	We have been in class for twenty minutes.
Since	Beginning of a period	We have been in class since 9 a.m.
Until	Continuance until a specific time	You will have until the end of class to finish the exam. Students have until December 1st to hand in their papers.
From-To	A specific time period	You will have from 9 a.m. to 10:15 a.m. to finish the exam.

» Prepositions of Location

The following prepositions are often used to discuss the location of a person or object.

Preposition	Use	Examples
At	General spaces Paper Groups of people	At the bus stop, at the movie theater. At the top/bottom of the page At the front/back of the class
In	Spaces with boundaries Bodies of water Lines	I am watching a movie in the theater. In the sea In a row/in a line
On	Surfaces Small islands Directions	On the wall/table On Maui On the left/right

Irregular Examples

Travel: on foot   in taxis/cars   on bikes/boats/public transportation
Corner: in a room corner   at/on a street corner

» Prepositions of Space

The following are common prepositions to explain where an object or a person is located.

Above	Around	Beyond	Near	Through
Across	Behind	By	Nearby	Toward
Against	Below	Down	Next to	Under
Ahead of	Beneath	From	On top of	Underneath
Along	Beside	In front of	Outside (of)	Up
Among	Between	Inside	Over	Within

Students need to also be aware of how prepositions are used with media.

The song was on the radio.   He listens to the radio every day.
I saw a program on television.   I read the article on the Internet.
I read the essay in a book/newspaper/magazine.

Activity 1

Complete the following sentences.

1. Are your children _____ the festival?

2. There is a beautiful picture _____ the wall.

3. I am _____ school, _____ the classroom, _____ the fourth floor.

4. _____ as long as I can remember, that elderly man has lived _____ that house _____ the corner of the street.

5. I missed my favorite program _____ television because I was reading a very exciting part _____ my book, so I had to watch the show later _____ the Internet.

Activity 2

Read the following sentences and insert the appropriate prepositions where necessary.

1. Jane is arriving January 26th 2 o'clock the afternoon.

2. It snows here every year December, so we always go outside and play the snow Christmas Day.

3. Michael came here foot, but because the flood, he had to leave a boat.

4. Frankie started working her company 2019.

5. Jill began working the project yesterday.

6. 2003, the students have eaten the cafeteria lunchtime. However, before there was a cafeteria, the students usually ate the large leafy trees.

7. When the taxis are a line, you have to take the taxi that is the others.

8. The students the back the class should write their names the top the page.

9. The moment, he is Jeju Island, but because he is afraid fish the water, he is spending all his time his hotel swimming pool.

10. You have 10 a.m. 11 a.m. to complete the exam. Please write all the information the boxes provided. Keep your eyes the paper, and do not look the papers the students sitting you.

11. A year, a burglar has been breaking buildings late night, and stealing jewelry locked cases. One night, a police officer heard a noise, and investigated. The burglar heard him, so he jumped a window and a truck. The police officer saw the truck's number, and caught the criminal.

4

Conditionals

Conditionals are used to show cause and effect relationships. They are complex sentences which consist of an "if" (sometimes "when") subordinating clause and a "main" independent clause.

Type	Construction	Examples
Type 0 Usual, habitual, or scientific fact	**If/When**: present simple **Main**: present simple	When I come to school, I take the bus. If I drink tea, I drink green tea. When water reaches 71 degrees at the top of Mt. Everest, it boils.
Type 1 Possible, likely to happen in the near future	**If**: present simple **Main**: will + base verb	If the weather is warm, we will go swimming. If I have an "A" average, I will get a scholarship. If the situation continues, profits will decrease.
Type 2 Unreal, unlikely to happen in the present	**If**: past simple **Main**: would* + base verb	If aliens attacked, I would fight them. If I were you, I would not do that. If I saw a burglary, I would call the police.
Type 3 Impossible past, regrets, imagining a different reality based on a different past	**If**: past perfect **Main**: would have + past participle	If aliens had attacked, I would have fought them. If I had been you, I would not have done that. If I had seen a burglary, I would have called the police.

*In Type 2 or 3 conditionals, "would" can be replaced with "might" (possibility) or "could" (option/ability).

Grammar Tip

In some cases, more than one type can be used to show different meanings.

Examples:
If I become the President, I will lower taxes. (a candidate in an election)
If I became the President, I would lower taxes. (regular people)

If our team wins, we will all cheer. (optimistic)
If our team won, we would all cheer. (pessimistic)

Grammar Tip

Second Conditional

When using the second conditional in the first person, use "were" instead of "was."
Example: If I were you, I would apply for the position.

Activity 1

Identify the following conditionals, and answer the questions.

1. When you exercise, what kind of exercise do you do? Type: 0 / 1 / 2 / 3

When I exercise, I play basketball.

2. If you were a horse, how would your life be different? Type: 0 / 1 / 2 / 3

3. If there is Asian dust tomorrow, will you go hiking? Type: 0 / 1 / 2 / 3

4. If you moved to another country, where would you want to live? Type: 0 / 1 / 2 / 3

5. If you get a job this vacation, what kind of work will you do? Type: 0 / 1 / 2 / 3

6. When you feel sad, how do you make yourself feel happy again? Type: 0 / 1 / 2 / 3

7. If you meet your friends this weekend, where will you go? Type: 0 / 1 / 2 / 3

8. If you saw a murder being committed, what would you do? Type: 0 / 1 / 2 / 3

9. If North Korea had won the Korean War, how would life have been different?
Type: 0 / 1 / 2 / 3

10. If you had failed the college entrance exam ten times, what would you have done?
Type: 0 / 1 / 2 / 3

_____

11. If you found a wallet filled with money on the street, what would you do with it?
Type: 0 / 1 / 2 / 3

_____

12. When you have a cold, what do you do to get better? Type: 0 / 1 / 2 / 3

_____

13. If you had been born 100 years ago, how would your life have been different?
Type: 0 / 1 / 2 / 3

_____

14. If you saw your friend cheat on a test, what would you do? Type: 0 / 1 / 2 / 3

_____

Activity 2

On a separate piece of paper, make your own Type 0–3 conditionals for another classmate to answer.

Activity 3

Choose one of the topics from Activity 1, and write a paragraph on the topic.

5 Modal auxiliary verbs

Modal verbs modify other verbs to show permission, ability, possibility, and obligation.

» Permission/Request

Can	Informal – question	Can I have some water?
May	Formal – question	May I borrow your pen?
Could	Formal – question	Could I use your phone?
Would	Formal/polite – question or statement	Would you like a drink? I would like a glass of water.

» Ability

Can/cannot	Present ability	He can ski. He cannot surf.
Could/could not	Past ability Option – polite or ability	He could ski when he was young. We could ski, or we could snowboard.

» Possibility

May/may not	Moderate future possibility	The bus may be here in five minutes.
Might/might not	Moderate present possibility Moderate future possibility	The bus might be here soon. The bus might be here in five minutes.
Should/should not	Stronger possibility	The bus should be here soon.
Must/must not	Certainty	The bus must be here by now.
Will/will not	Future certainty	The bus will arrive at 9 pm.

» Suggestions/Obligation

Should/should not	Recommendation Duty (Can be refused)	You should eat at that new restaurant. I should go to the party, but I am sick.
Ought to / ought not to	Necessity (ethical)	Leaders ought to set a good example.
Must	Necessity (personal feeling)	I must study harder if I want to pass.
Must not	Negative law	Passengers must not bring guns on planes.
Have to * (Need to)	Necessity (from an outside source - parents, teachers, boss, law, reason)	My teacher said I have to study harder. I have to write a quiz today. Korean drivers have to wear seatbelts.
Do not have to *	Not necessary	Cyclists do not have to wear a helmet.
(Had) better (not) *	Warning	You better write the quiz, or you will fail. You better not swim in shark infested water.

*These phrases are not modal verbs, but they are often used in a similar way as modal verbs.

Activity 1

Fill in the blanks with the appropriate word(s).

Hyun Gee has a weight problem. He knows that he _____ eat fresh fruits and vegetables instead of instant or fatty food, and he _____ eat healthy food because he lives in the countryside; however, he prefers to eat junk food every day. Because his father died early from a heart attack, he has always known that he _____ have heart problems in the future. However, yesterday he went to the doctor who told him that he _____ start eating better because his health is in serious trouble. In fact, the doctor said that he _____ lose weight immediately, and he _____ eat any more fast food, or he _____ have a heart attack within the next few months. Needless to say, now Hyun Gee knows how serious the situation is, he also feels that he _____ lose weight.

When Ga Eun started her job, she was told that she _____ work overtime unless she wanted to do extra work. She was also told that she _____ be able to get a promotion within six months like more than two thirds of her other coworkers. However, she now realizes that if her boss asks her if she _____ work overtime, it really means that she _____ work late regardless of whether or not she has other plans. She now also knows that she _____ never complain about her work hours because then she most certainly _____ get a promotion.

Waiter: "Good evening, Sir. _____ I take your order?"

Customer: "Yes, I _____ like to order red wine and steak with a side order of salad."

W: "I'm sorry, Sir, but tonight we _____ serve that dish because we are out of steak. You _____ order grilled chicken, or you _____ have oysters instead."

C: "Unfortunately, I _____ eat oysters because I'm allergic to them, so I guess I _____ order the grilled chicken."

W: "_____ you like to order dessert now?"

C: "I _____ have dessert later, but I'm not sure yet."

W: "Very well, Sir. I _____ be back in a moment with your wine."

Activity 2

Using the modal verb and conditional lessons, answer the questions in full conditional sentences.

Example: Hyun Young got lost driving to the beach. What could she have done to have avoided getting lost?

Possible Answer: If I had been Hyun Young, I would have used my GPS.

1. Hyun Seok lost a million won gambling at the casino. What could he have done with that money?

_____

2. A business owner needs to cut costs. What usually happens in this situation?

_____

3. Elizabeth did not like her new boss, so she quit her job immediately. Are there any other ways she might have solved her problem?

_____

4. Hwa Kyung just found a diamond ring on the street. If you were her, what would you do?

_____

5. A student went out drinking the night before his exam. What usually happens in this situation?

_____

6. Seung Ho is watching two teenagers beat up a homeless man. If you were him, what would you do?

_____

7. Min Kyoung has a blind date tomorrow. What do you think might happen?

_____

8. A twelve-year-old boy runs away from home. What might happen to him?

_____

9. Young Jun forgot to lock the door when he left home. What could happen to his house?

_____

Adjectives

Adjectives are descriptive words which modify or give more details about nouns.

Example: I have a car.
Example: I have a shiny new black car.

In the above example, the adjectives are in front of the noun; however, adjectives can follow nouns if you use sense verbs (smell, taste, look, etc.) or verbs of being (be, seem).

Example: The car looked shiny and new.

> **Grammar Tip**
>
> As in most English grammar rules, there are some exceptions to adjective order, most notably, words, titles, or phrases which have been influenced by French.
>
> **Example**: Boutros Boutros Ghali is a former Secretary General of the United Nations.

» Adjective Order

When using more than one adjective, it is important to know the order in which they should be placed.

Determiner	Opinion	Physical Description					Origin	Material	Type/Purpose
		Size	Quality	Shape	Age	Color			
three	funny	big	shiny	flat	old	red	Kenyan	wood	baseball
a	beautiful	small	smooth	square	new	blue	Western	gold	computer
some	sweet	tiny	rough	round	one year old	pink	British	glass	sports
many	terrifying	huge	weathered	spherical	vintage	white	Cartier	leather	homemade

> **Grammar Tip**
>
> In general, writers should not use more than three adjectives (not including the determiner) in a row to describe a noun.
>
> **Examples**: Three funny old baseball players were teaching children how to play the game.
> A shiny new gold watch was lying on the ground.
> Some sweet British grandmothers raised money to help homeless dogs.
> Many terrifying huge white dogs attacked me.

Grammar Tip

If there are two adjectives of the same type, the order does not matter, but they should be separated by a comma.

Example: The crunchy, sweet cookies were homemade.
Example: The sweet, crunchy cookies were homemade.

Activity 1

Identify the adjectives in the sentence and their type. Then correct the sentence if it is in the wrong order.

1. The actor famous lived in a brick modest simple home.

_____

2. Yoon Jin's loud annoying parrot lives in a black metal enormous cage.

_____

3. Paul told his friends about the ferocious puppy Dalmatian.

_____

4. The ancient German castle sat empty in the open field.

_____

5. Donna brought back silk from India flowing soft.

_____

6. A black ugly old cat scared me when it jumped from the window to the ground.

_____

7. I could not study because there were noisy four women laughing loudly.

_____

8. Ainsley's fiancé gave her a ring diamond expensive Tiffany.

_____

9. These kiwis green New Zealand are both tangy and sweet.

_____

10. The students journalism decided to start new campus a newspaper.

_____

» Adjective Clauses

Adjective clauses are dependent clauses which modify nouns to give more information or to clarify a noun.

Example: Blizzards are dangerous storms which include high winds and heavy snowfall.

Relative Pronouns

Adjective clauses always require relative pronouns. The following chart organizes the type of relative pronoun, and its place or function in a sentence.

Function	People	Things	Place	Time	Explanation
Subject	Who, that	Which, that			
Object	That, whom	Which, that	Where, which	When	What, why
Possessive	Whose	Whose, of which			

Example:

Is that the person who stole your wallet? (subject)

Is that the person whom you mugged? (object)

Is that the person whose wallet was stolen? (possessive)

🔆 Grammar Tip

When talking about a place, "which" is more formal than "where," and "whom" is generally more formal than "that" in English sentences.

Example: "There is the place where she met her husband." (informal)
Example: "There is the place at which she met her husband" (formal)

Similarly, "that" is more often used in informal English than "who" (for people) or "which" (for things). However, "that" is the preferred relative pronoun in two cases.

1. Indefinite pronouns
Example: I told him to pack **everything** that fits in the suitcases.

2. Nouns modified by superlatives
Example: He is **the fastest** runner that the world has ever seen.

Types of Adjective Clauses

There are two types of adjective clauses, the defining relative clause and the non-defining relative clause.

Defining Relative Clause

Example: A farmer is a person who grows crops and raises livestock.

Non-Defining Relative Clause

Example: Julie's farm, which had been owned by her family for a century, was sold last week.

 Grammar Tip

Commas are not usually used after the relative pronoun in the defining relative clause. However, if additional information is given in the non-defining relative clause that is not necessary to understand the meaning of the subject of the sentence, then commas are necessary.

My sister, who lives in Ireland, is studying medicine. (one sister)
My sister who lives in Ireland is a student. My sister who lives in Hong Kong is a business person.

Activity 1

Choose the correct relative pronoun for formal writing.

1. Is Lisa the girl _____ dress was ruined?

2. Do you know the actor _____ is the villain in this movie?

3. Eun Joo, _____ was falsely accused of murder, spent ten years
   in the jail _____ is located just outside of the city.

4. Is she the one _____ you are going to invite to the party?

5. He is the youngest chef _____ has ever graduated from this cooking academy.

6. Do you know the reason _____ so few people came to this event?

7. George has a car _____ is always breaking down, but he can take it to his uncle's
   repair shop _____ is cheaper than other places.

Activity 2

Add commas to the following sentences where appropriate.

1. Glenn is a boy who loves horses.

2. They hired the quiet woman whom the boss interviewed last week.

3. The company which is located on the other side of the street has 532 employees.

4. Gregor's Hamburgers which is the largest restaurant chain in the city was established in 1962.

5. The man whose leg was hurt in a car accident was taken to the hospital by ambulance.

6. Where is the good looking guy whom you want to invite to the party?

7. Robson Motors which is the top ranking car company in the country had to recall thousands of cars last week because of engine problems.

8. The textbook which is on top of Yong Hee's desk is the textbook for this class.

9. *Gray's Anatomy* which has been an extremely important medical textbook for the past 150 years was written by Henry Gray.

10. The house which is located at the end of the street is mine.

Activity 3

Write your own definitions for the following nouns using adjective clauses.

1. Bees

_____

2. Mothers

_____

3. Passports

_____

4. Love

_____

5. Education

_____

7

Active vs. Passive Voice

One of the first lessons students learn when they begin to study English sentence structure is English sentences are usually ordered this way: subject + verb + object. The subject performs the action, the verb is the action, and the object is the recipient of the action.

> subject   object
> **Example**: The **cat ate** the **mouse**.
>   verb

This sentence structure is called "active voice," and it is the preferred order for many kinds of writing, especially in the humanities. Nevertheless, a different kind of sentence structure called "passive voice" is also necessary in certain instances.

> **Example**: The mouse was eaten by the cat.
> auxiliary verb (form of "to be") + main verb (past participle) + (by) = passive voice

In the above example, the object and subject switch places without changing the underlying meaning of the sentence.

Passive use is the preferable form of sentence structure in the following instances:

Situation	Explanation	Example
Scientific reports and papers	Passive voice is considered more objective in science.	Cancerous cells were found in the samples.
Emphasizing an object	Sometimes emphasizing the object is more dramatic, or authors want to emphasize the effect instead of the cause.	Millions of people were killed by the government during the bloody conflict.
Uncertain, unclear, or unknown subject	In some cases, the subject is either unknown or unimportant in the sentence.	The windows were broken around midnight.

💡 Grammar Tip

The auxiliary verb (to be) changes depending on the time period and amount.

The prisoner **was brought** in yesterday.
The prisoners **are being brought** in at this moment.
The prisoner **will be brought** in tomorrow.

Activity 1

Change the following active sentences into passive sentences.

1. Most Koreans eat *kimchi*.

_____

2. Heavy rain caused a landslide.

_____

3. A massive earthquake and tsunami damaged the Fukushima Daiichi nuclear plant in 2011.

_____

4. Sir Edmund Hillary and Tenzing Norgay were the first people to successfully reach the summit of Mt. Everest in 1953.

_____

5. Kim Yuna won the gold medal in women's figure skating at the 2010 Winter Olympic Games.

_____

Activity 2

Change the following passive sentences into active sentences. If there is no clear actor in the original sentence, use common sense to determine the subject in the active sentence.

1. He was hired for the new position.

_____

2. The bathrooms are cleaned at around 1 pm.

_____

3. The student was failed for plagiarizing her essay.

_____

4. Hangul was developed in the 15th century.

_____

5. English is taught in this class.

_____

6. Lee Myung-bak was elected as the President of the Republic of Korea in 2008.

_____

8 Comparatives and Superlatives

Writers often use adjectives or descriptive words to describe the nouns they are using. Sometimes when there is more than one noun, writers want to talk about differences between the nouns by using comparatives and superlatives.

Comparatives compare two adjectives describing nouns while superlatives show the greatest degree of a characteristic.

Examples:
This dress is more expensive than that dress. (comparative)
This dress is the most expensive in the store. (superlative)

» Adjective Modification

Adjectives are modified as comparatives and superlatives based on the number of syllables or beats in the word.

Examples:
Beautiful - Beau/ti/ful (3 syllables)
More/less beautiful (comparative)
The most/the least beautiful (superlative)

Sweet (1 syllable)
Sweeter (comparative)
Sweetest (superlative)

Learners should note that their first language often affects their second, and this can lead to an atypical number of syllables. For example, Korean speakers often pronounce cute (one syllable) as kju-teu (two syllables). Learners are therefore advised to familiarize themselves with typical pronunciation before modifying adjectives.

Example:
Cute: Typical English: [kjuːt] (1 syllable) versus Korean English [kʲʊtʰɯ] (kju-teu: 2 syllables)

Therefore, students need to make sure they are sounding out syllables with English pronunciation before they modify adjectives.

» Constructing Comparatives and Superlatives

Rule	Comparative Form	Superlative Form
1 syllable ending in "e" fine, wide	Add "r" finer, wider	Add "st" finest, widest
1 syllable ending in 1 vowel and 1 consonant hot, sad	Double the consonant + "er" hotter, sadder	Double the consonant +est hottest, saddest
1 syllable ending in more than 1 consonant or vowel strange, cool	Add + "er" stranger, cooler	Add "est" strangest, coolest
2 syllables ending in "y" silly, funny	"y" ⇨ "i" + "er" sillier, funnier	"y" ⇨ "i" + "est" silliest, funniest
2 syllables or more (not ending in "y") beautiful, expensive	Add "more" more beautiful, more expensive	Add "most" most beautiful, most expensive

Word	Comparative Form	Superlative form
clever	cleverer/more clever	cleverest/most clever
gentle	gentler/more gentle	gentlest/most gentle
friendly	friendlier/more friendly	friendliest/most friendly
quiet	quieter/ more quiet	quietest/most quiet
simple	simpler/more simple	simplest/most simple

The following adjectives are irregular and do not follow the previously given rules.

Word	Comparative Form	Superlative Form
good	better	best
bad	worse	worst
far	farther	farthest
little	less	least
many	more	most

Signpost See page 116 for information about the definite article and superlatives.

Activity 1

Read the following passages and modify them as appropriate.

At first glance, it does not seem that Hyea Su is a unique student. She is smart, but there are other students who are smart than her. Similarly, when playing sports, she is not the fast or the slow student, and half of the class can run far than her in little time than she can run. However, Hyea Su is a very funny girl, and she tells the good jokes and stories her friends have ever heard. Her classmates think that one day she may become famous comedian in Korea because of her great sense of humor.

Andy wanted to buy a new car. He was not looking for the cheap car or the expensive car but for a mid-priced vehicle. Initially, the car salesperson showed him a red car and a black car. The red car accelerated fast and had good features than the black car, but the black car was many fuel efficient and had a sleek design than the other car. Andy could not decide which car was good. Finally, the salesperson showed him a white car. It was a bit expensive than the other two, but in every other way, it was the good of the three cars. In the end, Andy drove home happy in his brand new white car.

Using Non-English Words in English

What Is the Difference Between a Sundae and *Sundae*?

Using italics helps the reader to understand the difference between an English term and a word from another language. Using Korean, Chinese, or words from any other language is perfectly acceptable in English assignments as long as the word is written and explained properly.

Step 1: Romanize the word.
Words written in other scripts need to be written in Roman characters.

비빔밥 → bibimbap
月饼 → yue bing

Step 2: Italics and capitalization
Non-English general nouns need to be italicized and left in lower case letters if they have not been accepted into the English language.

bibimbap → *bibimbap*
yue bing → *yue bing*

If these words are written by hand, they should be underlined.
bibimbap → bibimbap

Proper nouns should not be italicized, and the first letter of each word should be capitalized.
Seoul → Seoul
kim eun jee → Kim Eun Jee, Kim Eunjee, Kim Eun Ji, or Kim Eunji

Step 3: Define and incorporate into a sentence
Writers should never assume their readers know non-English words; therefore, general nouns need to be explained or defined the first time they are used. Non-English words should also conform to English grammar rules.

Bibimbap is a Korean dish that consists of mixed rice, vegetables, egg, and red pepper paste.
Yue bing is a traditional Chinese dessert that is eaten during the Mid-Autumn Festival.

⊕ Grammar Tip

If a non-English word has an easy translation, use the appropriate English word.

She wore a beautiful *jinju* necklace. → She wore a beautiful pearl necklace.

Activity 1

Change the following words into Roman script and decide if these words should be italicized (underlined) or capitalized.

막걸리	고추장	고시원	김치찌개
삼겹살	설날	호떡	대구시
대구	성균관대학교	上海	餃子

Activity 2

Now use simple adjective clauses to define these words in a sentence.

막걸리 _____

고추장 _____

삼겹살 _____

김치찌개 _____

호떡 _____

설날 _____

餃子 _____

Signpost See page 134–136 for more information on simple adjective clauses.

Activity 3

Using the space provided, rewrite one of the following paragraphs using the steps previously covered.

추석 is a wonderful way to experience unique aspects of Korean culture. For instance, food is a very important part of the holiday. For dinner, Koreans usually eat 불고기 and 잡채. They also eat 송편 or drink 식혜 after the main meal. Many families also engage in tradition when they perform 차례 by a special table set with offerings of food such as 밥, 과일, and 생선. Sometimes families will even dress in 한복 for this activity. Finally, some Koreans still enjoy watching 씨름 matches during the vacation period. Thus, 추석 is a great way to understand traditional Korean culture.

北京 is a great place to travel on vacation. First, 毛澤東's tomb is an important place to visit to understand the history of China, and 万里长城 is located close to the city, allowing visitors to visit it easily. In addition, many kinds of food are found throughout the city. 北京烤鸭 is the most famous. However, 烙饼 is also a quick snack tourists can enjoy. Finally, no trip is complete without a trip to the 京剧. Therefore, if tourists want a fun-filled destination where they can eat local delicacies, they should visit 北京.

_____

_____

_____

_____

_____

_____

_____

_____

_____

_____

_____

10 Paraphrasing and Summarizing

In academic writing, writers often integrate information from other sources in order to support their own ideas and opinions. Paraphrasing and summarizing are ways of incorporating ideas from other sources without using the exact words.

What Is Paraphrasing?

Paraphrasing is rewording and rearranging the content of text without changing the meaning or dramatically altering the length. It is a useful alternative to a direct quotation when using information from another source, and it is a valuable skill that is used in the writing process.

Example:
Original text (21 words)

In his prime, soccer star Wayne Rooney was a machine designed for sport. His stocky, powerful physique made him more powerful than his opponents.

Paraphrased version (23 words)

At his peak, Wayne Rooney—a famous soccer player—had a powerful body, which made him a stronger soccer player than the players he competed against.

Summarized version (10 words)
Wayne Rooney's powerful body made him a soccer legend.

How to Paraphrase

There are three main steps in the processes of paraphrasing:

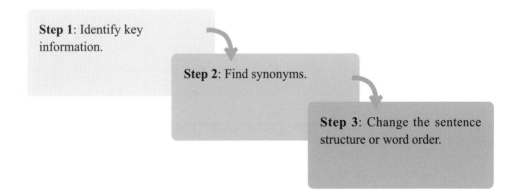

Step 1: Identify key information.

Step 2: Find synonyms.

Step 3: Change the sentence structure or word order.

Example 2:

Original text

An article in *GQ* magazine reports that actor David DeMotto is considering retirement from the movie business due to an undisclosed medical condition.

Step 1: Identify key information.

Read the text carefully and highlight or underline the important words to change.

An article in *GQ* magazine **reports** that **actor** David DeMotto is **considering** retirement from the **movie business** due to an **undisclosed medical condition**.

Step 2: Find synonyms.

Report	rumour, state, disclose, reveal
Actor	film star, thespian, performer, player
Considering	thinking about, contemplating, planning on
Movie business	film industry, acting
Undisclosed	unnamed, unidentified, secret
Medical condition	health problem, personal reason

New sentence:

An article in *GQ* magazine reveals that film star David DeMotto is thinking about retirement from the film industry due to health problems.

Step 3: Change the sentence structure.

Paraphrase 1:

Film star David DeMotto is thinking about retirement from the film industry due to health problems, according to an article in *GQ* magazine.

Paraphrase 2:

Due to health problems, film star David DeMotto is thinking about retirement from the film industry, according to an article in *GQ* magazine.

Signpost See page 13–20 for more information on sentence types.

Activity 1

Rewrite the following sentences by following steps 1–3.

1. The little boy named Sam was very nervous about his test; as a result, he vomited.

    _____

    _____

2. The rural school could not afford to buy new computers, for they were not cheap.

    _____

    _____

3. Although Nak Kyun stayed up all night writing his essay, he had too many grammar mistakes to get a good mark.

    _____

    _____

4. Children between the ages of 9 and 12 study for an average of five hours every week outside of normal school hours.

    _____

    _____

5. It is against the law for teachers to use corporal punishment in schools in New Zealand.

    _____

    _____

6. Learning English is very important for entrance into good schools and more opportunities in the workplace.

    _____

    _____

7. *FourFourTwo* Magazine described Park Ji-sung as one of the best Asian players to have played in the English Premier League.

    _____

    _____

8. South Korean group BTS became the first K-pop group to top the U.S. Billboard 200 charts.

    _____

    _____

What Is Summarizing?

Like paraphrasing, summarizing involves rewording and rearranging the content of a text without changing the meaning, but the writer dramatically reduces the length to provide an overview of the original text. This is particularly useful when a writer wishes to focus on the main idea without including examples, statistics, and details.

How to summarize

There are three main steps in the processes of summarizing:

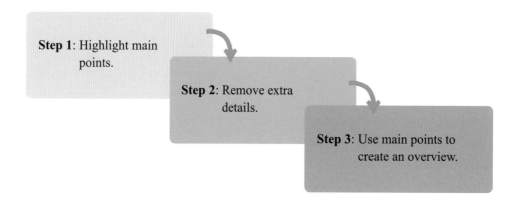

Step 1: Highlight main points.

Step 2: Remove extra details.

Step 3: Use main points to create an overview.

Example:
Original text (118 words)

> In his prime, soccer star Wayne Rooney was a machine designed for sports. His stocky, powerful physique made him more powerful than his opponents. At a height of 176 cm, Rooney had a low center of gravity, which enabled him to change direction quickly at pace, and outmaneuver bigger defenders. His upper body strength was a considerable asset, and allowed him to hold-off other players while controlling the ball. Although not gifted with electric pace, Rooney's leg strength allowed him to kick the ball with remarkable force, which is a great asset as a striker. Because of these physical attributes and never-say-die attitude, Rooney is considered one of the best players to have played the game.

Step 1: Highlight the main points

> In his prime, soccer star **Wayne Rooney** was a machine designed for sports. His stocky, powerful physique made him **more powerful than his opponents.** At a height of 176 cm, Rooney had a **low center of gravity,** which enabled him to change direction quickly at pace, and outmaneuver bigger defenders. His **upper body strength** was a considerable asset, and allowed him to hold off other players while controlling the ball. Although not gifted with electric pace, Rooney's **leg strength** allowed him to kick the ball with remarkable force, which is a great asset as a striker. Because of these physical attributes and never-say-die attitude, Rooney is considered **one of the best players** to have played the game.

Step 2: Remove extra details

Wayne Rooney
more powerful than his opponents
low centre of gravity
upper body strength
leg strength
one of the best players

Step 3: Use the main points to write an overview

Summarized version (9 words)

Wayne Rooney's powerful body made him a soccer legend.

Activity 2

Now try to summarize the following information into one sentence using steps 1–3.

In 2018, South Korea's birthrate fell to 0.98 children per woman [1]. This was a fall of 8.7 % from the previous year [2]. Most people aged 20–44 were single in 2018, and most of the single people wished to remain single [3], claiming that they lack emotional capacity, money, and time to date [2].

References

[1] The Economist, "South Korea's fertility rate falls to a record low," *The Economist*, Aug. 2019.

[2] J. Kwon and J. Yeung, "South Korea's fertility rate falls to record low," *CNN*, Aug. 29, 2019. Accessed: Jan. 18, 2024. [Online]. Available: https://edition.cnn.com/2019/08/29/asia/south-korea-fertility-intl-hnk-trnd/index.html

[3] S. Lee, "2018 National Survey on Fertility, Family Health and Welfare," 2019. https://www.kihasa.re.kr/english/publications/eng_research/view.do?menuId=71&tid=34&bid=87&ano=948 (accessed Jan. 18, 2024).

_____

_____

_____

_____

Although Korean adults have one of the lowest levels of obesity in the world, Korean children are getting heavier. A recent study from the Institute for Childhood Nutrition shows 1 in 10 children are obese, and a larger number are overweight. Because of the university entrance exam, even young students spend an increasing amount of time sitting in their chairs studying at home, at afterschool programs, and at their regular public schools. In addition, instead of a diet full of fresh vegetables and fruit, children today eat more junk or instant food than ever before. Ramyeon, chips, frozen pre-prepared meals, and hamburgers or French fries have now replaced well balanced, homemade meals for children.

_____

_____

_____

_____

_____

_____

Activity 2

Use the three summarizing steps to change each paragraph into one sentence.

Homeschooling

There are several different reasons why students are homeschooled. Some religious families feel that their children need an education that is more focused on their beliefs. Other parents are worried about negative influences in public schools such as smoking, drugs, bullying, or other forms of violence. There are also children who do not fit in with the regular school system because they are either gifted children who learn faster than regular students or because they have learning disabilities or learn slower than other students. Thus, there is no one reason why parents decide to homeschooled their children.

_____

_____

_____

_____

_____

Because homeschooling is so different from public schools, some people have concerns about children learning at home. Unlike mainstream schools where children are exposed to a diversity of people and opinions from different teachers and interacting with other students, homeschooled children have only their parents' perspectives or the curriculum's perspective, which was probably chosen by the parents. In addition, children might not be well socialized with mainstream society. As a result, homeschooled children might not be able to fit well into the rest of the community later in life.

_____

_____

_____

_____

_____

Despite these problems, there are also benefits to homeschooling. First, children who are very talented or are experiencing learning disabilities can learn at their own pace at home. Children who excel at languages, science, or other subjects can devote more time to their area or areas of interest, and those students may one day be great linguists or scientists because of their extra studies; on the other hand, students who are struggling in one area can devote more time to reading skills, mathematics, or whatever subject they need to improve. The second advantage is that children can have a closer relationship with their parents because they spend much more time with their parents than in the traditional education system. Likewise, parents who teach their children are much more involved in their education, and they can help guide their children in life and education.

_____

_____

_____

_____

_____

_____

💡 Tip

If paraphrasing or summarizing from another source, you must include an in-text citation in order to indicate clearly where you found the original information. See 157 for more information on in-text citations.

11 Scientific Vocabulary and Collocations

It is difficult to imagine an area of language learning that is more important than vocabulary. Many studies, e.g. [1], [2], [3], [4], [5], [6, p. 41], show that vocabulary size correlates with proficiency in overall language, reading, listening, writing, speaking, and grammar. In our context, we are developing proficiency in scientific writing, so we should consider scientific vocabulary. In some disciplines, e.g., anatomy, almost one in every three words is technical [7], so learning this is clearly important for writing.

All technical language use requires specific vocabulary that is unlikely to be learnt when studying general language use. For example, the *Medical Academic Word List* shows that *insulin* is at least the 2090th most frequent word in medical research articles [8], while *VocabProfiler* shows that there are at least 5000 more frequent words in general English [9]. Clearly different words are more frequent (and therefore likely more useful) in different academic fields [10], so references for useful lists are provided here. Use your library to find and download the articles which you feel most suit your needs. The word lists are often buried amidst the articles, which explain how they were compiled. If you wish to skip the explanations, simply scroll until you reach the lists.

References

[1]   S. Hazenberg and J. H. Hulstijn, "Defining a minimal receptive second-language vocabulary for non-native university students: An empirical investigation," *Appl. Linguist.*, vol. 17, no. 2, pp. 145–163, 1996.

[2]   B. Laufer, "Reading in a foreign language: How does L2 lexical knowledge interact with the reader's general academic ability?," *J. Res. Read.*, vol. 15, no. 2, pp. 95–103, 1992.

[3]   J. Milton, J. Wade, and N. Hopkins, "Aural word recognition and oral competence in English as a foreign language," in *Insights into non-native vocabulary teaching and learning*, R. Chacón-Beltrán, C. Abello-Contesse, and M. del Mar Torreblanca-López, Eds. Multilingual Matters, 2010, pp. 83–98.

[4]   D. D. Qian, "Assessing the roles of depth and breadth of vocabulary knowledge in reading comprehension," *Can. Mod. Lang. Rev.*, vol. 56, no. 2, pp. 282–308, 1999.

[5]   L. S. Staehr, "Vocabulary size and the skills of listening, reading and writing," *Lang. Learn. Journal2*, vol. 38, no. 2, pp. 139–152, 2008.

[6]   K. J. Zimmerman, "The role of vocabulary size in assessing second language," Brigham Young University, Provo, 2004.

[7]   T. M. Chung and P. Nation, "Technical vocabulary in specialised texts," *Read. a Foreign Lang.*, vol. 15, no. 2, pp. 103–116, 2003.

[8]   J. Wang, S. Liang, and G. Ge, "Establishment of a Medical Academic Word List," *English Specif. Purp.*, vol. 27, no. 4, pp. 442–458, 2008.

[9]   T. M. Cobb, "Compleat web VP! [Computer program]," *Compleat Lexical Tutor*. Université du Québec à Montréal, Montréal.

[10]   A. Coxhead, "A new academic word list," *TESOL Q.*, vol. 34, no. 2, pp. 213–238, 2000.

General Academic Word Lists

Probably the most famous list of academic vocabulary is the *Academic Word List* (AWL) [1]. This was compiled by counting the words in journal articles from many different academic fields. The words in the *General Service List* (GSL: a list of the most common 2000 words in general English) [2] were then removed, determining which 520 other words occur most frequently in academic English writing. Later, a larger, more recent list of academic text was used to compile the *Academic Vocabulary List* (AVL) of 500 words which occur frequently in academic English writing [3].

References

[1]   A. Coxhead, "A new academic word list," *TESOL Q.*, vol. 34, no. 2, pp. 213–238, 2000.

[2]   M. West, "Interim report on vocabulary selection for the teaching of English as a foreign language," in *Interim report on vocabulary selection for the teaching of English as a foreign language*, L. Faucett, M. P. West, H. E. Palmer, and E. L. Thorndike, Eds. London: P.S. King & Son, 1936.

[3]   D. Gardner and M. Davies, "A new academic vocabulary list," *Appl. Linguist.*, vol. 35, no. 3, pp. 305–327, 2014.

Collocations

Collocations are combinations of words that often occur together, e.g., *stark contrast*, a *great deal of*, and *profound implications*. When learning vocabulary, it is important to learn collocations, which are learnt and recalled as fixed phrases. For example, most speakers retrieve "Thank you very much." from memory as one phrase, not as four words. Learning collocations can thus make vocabulary use easier, lessening the mind's workload. Collocations account for 21% of academic text, and 70% of academic collocations are based on noun phrases (e.g. *the nature of the*) and prepositional phrases (e.g. *as a result of*) [1].

An *Academic Formulas List* (AFL) was compiled from collocations occurring in written and spoken academic English [2]. Focusing only on written language, the *Academic Collocations List* (ACL) was built by reviewing statistical analysis of academic articles [3]. Whereas most lists are based on academic articles, two lists compile collocations appearing in university textbooks: [4], and in particular for engineering and business, [5].

References

[1]   D. Biber, S. Conrad, and V. Cortes, "If you look at...: Lexical bundles in university teaching and textbooks," *Appl. Linguist.*, vol. 25, no. 3, pp. 371–405, Sep. 2004.

[2]   R. Simpson-Vlach and N. C. Ellis, "An academic formulas list: New methods in phraseology research," *Appl. Linguist.*, vol. 31, no. 4, pp. 487–512, 2010.

[3]   K. Ackermann and Y. H. Chen, "Developing the Academic Collocation List (ACL) - A corpus-driven and expert-judged approach," *J. English Acad. Purp.*, vol. 12, no. 4, pp. 235–247, 2013.

[4]   W. Hsu, "The most frequent opaque formulaic sequences in English-medium college textbooks," *System*, vol. 47, pp. 146–161, 2014.

[5]   D. C. Wood and R. Appel, "Multiword constructions in first year business and engineering university textbooks and EAP textbooks," *J. English Acad. Purp.*, vol. 15, pp. 1–13, 2014.

General Science

A science-specific word list [1] was compiled from scientific journals articles, with the vocabulary appearing in the GSL [2] and the AWL [3] removed, leaving 318 words that appeared frequently in scientific articles but less often in the arts. This list was formed from a relatively small sample of articles, but this remains perhaps the best available list based on a range of scientific research articles.

The *Science Textbook Word List* was formed from a review of 12 undergraduate level textbooks from various fields of science and engineering [4]. This is also from a relatively small sample of authors, but there are few available lists of general science vocabulary.

References

[1]   A. Coxhead and D. Hirsh, "A pilot science-specific word list," *Rev. française Linguist. appliquée*, vol. XII, no. 2, pp. 65–78, 2007.

[2]   M. West, "Interim report on vocabulary selection for the teaching of English as a foreign language," in *Interim report on vocabulary selection for the teaching of English as a foreign language*, L. Faucett, M. P. West, H. E. Palmer, and E. L. Thorndike, Eds. London: P.S. King & Son, 1936.

[3]   A. Coxhead, "A new academic word list," *TESOL Q.*, vol. 34, no. 2, pp. 213–238, 2000.

[4]   J. Veenstra and Y. Sato, "Creating an institution-specific science and engineering academic world list for university students," *J. Asia TEFL*, vol. 15, no. 1, pp. 148–166, 2018.

Agriculture

An agricultural vocabulary list of 102 academic words from agriculture research articles has been compiled [1]. This list overlaps with the GSL and the AWL, as some AWL words have specific agricultural meanings, while some GSL words have academic contexts in agriculture.

Reference

[1]   I. A. Martínez, S. C. Beck, and C. B. Panza, "Academic vocabulary in agriculture research articles: A corpus-based study," *English Specif. Purp.*, vol. 28, no. 3, pp. 183–198, 2009.

Biology, Mathematics and Physics

There is a list of biology, mathematics and physics vocabulary for secondary (middle) school students [1]. This is not ideal for university level study, but such lists have not yet been published for higher levels.

Reference

[1]   C. Green and J. Lambert, "Advancing disciplinary literacy through English for academic purposes: Discipline-specific wordlists, collocations and word families for eight secondary subjects," *J. English Acad. Purp.*, vol. 35, pp. 105–115, 2018.

Chemistry

The *Chemistry Academic Word List* (CAWL) lists 1400 words which occur frequently in chemistry journals [1]. The authors claim that students who learn these words will know enough words to read chemistry research articles.

Reference

[1]   L. Valipouri and H. Nassaji, "A corpus-based study of academic vocabulary in chemistry research articles," *J. English Acad. Purp.*, vol. 12, no. 4, pp. 248–263, 2013.

Computer Science

There is a short list of 100 non-AWL words which commonly occur in computer science research articles [1].

Reference

[1]   J. Lee and H. Lee, "Academic vocabulary in computer science research articles: A corpus-based study," *J. Adv. Res. Dyn. Control Syst.*, vol. 10, no. 14, pp. 382–389, 2018.

Engineering

An engineering word list for undergraduates who are beginning their studies has been compiled [1]. This list is based on foundation engineering textbooks, not on journals. There is also a vocabulary list from engineering textbooks, though not for undergraduate study [2].

References

[1]   J. Ward, "A basic engineering English word list for less proficient foundation engineering undergraduates," *English Specif. Purp.*, vol. 28, no. 3, pp. 170–182, 2009.

[2]   R. Watson Todd, "An opaque engineering word list: Which words should a teacher focus on?," *English Specif. Purp.*, vol. 45, pp. 31–39, 2017.

Medicine

The *Medical Academic Word List* is compiled from research articles [1], while another list of medical vocabulary is based on research articles and case histories [2].

References

[1]   J. Wang, S. Liang, and G. Ge, "Establishment of a Medical Academic Word List," *English Specif. Purp.*, vol. 27, no. 4, pp. 442–458, 2008.

[2]   P. Mungra and T. Canziani, "Lexicographic studies in medicine: Academic Word List for clinical case histories," *Rev. Ibérica*, vol. 25, pp. 39–62, 2013.

Learning Vocabulary

It is of course insufficient merely to read a list of words, hoping to learn it. Most second language learners are likely familiar with the two main levels of vocabulary learning: receptive and productive. Many people recognize words yet fail to use them. Productive knowledge is thus a deeper level of vocabulary acquisition. It is well-reported that most skills are learnt through repetition. For example, reading a book about driving will not enable you to drive a car. Even if you know how to change gear, only after many repetitions can it be performed smoothly. Similarly, with vocabulary learning, the word must be retrieved from memory, and used often to be learned. Students are therefore encouraged to practice using their newly-acquired technical vocabulary in their speaking and writing.

Some learners may wonder why words should be spoken. After all, this book is concerned with writing. It has been demonstrated that pronunciation is important when reading [1], and the 'inner voice' (speaking in our head, not through our mouth) is important for writing fluency [2]. It is thus more difficult to use a word if we do not know its pronunciation. Learners are therefore encouraged to learn words' pronunciation when studying vocabulary, and to practice using them in speech as well as in writing.

References

[1]   M. Daneman and M. Stainton, "Phonological recoding in silent reading," *1Journal Exp. Psychol. Learn. Mem. Cogn.*, vol. 17, no. 4, pp. 618–632, 1991.

[2]   N. A. Chenoweth and J. R. Hayes, "The inner voice in writing," *Writ. Commun.*, vol. 20, no. 1, pp. 99–118, 2003.

Research Skills

Students often hear that they should not plagiarize or copy someone else's work, but they do not always have the skills to avoid replicating previously published work. This section gives students practical skills to both avoid plagiarism and make their writing assignments stronger by incorporating outside evidence into their work. Students will first learn what plagiarism is and how they can correctly incorporate in-text citations and quotations. Finally, they will learn how to cite sources used in their writing.

This section covers:

- Research and Writing
- In-Text Citations
- Quotations
- Reference Lists
- Reference Management Software

Research and Writing

In academic writing, it is not enough just to provide your own ideas and opinions. Good academic writing involves the development of the writer's ideas with support from other credible authors and sources.

When writers provide information from other sources, they must provide the reader with proper documentation of all the information used. If writers take information without acknowledging it, they are guilty of plagiarism.

What Is Plagiarism?

Plagiarism is taking information and ideas from other sources and claiming them to be yours. By not acknowledging the source(s), the writer is committing literary theft.

In Example 1, Student A has taken information from the author H.J. Chang but has not acknowledged it. The writer is claiming that the idea is his/her own. This is plagiarism.

> **Example 1**: Culture influences a country's economic performance. A particular culture may produce people with certain behavioral traits.

In Example 2, the writer has cited the source, and the complete details will be available in the References at the end of the report.

> **Example 2**: Countries' economies are affected by culture, particular cultures causing certain behavioral traits [1].

Writers are also guilty of plagiarism if they attempt to paraphrase too closely (put into your own words) information from another source. In Example 3, while the writer does not use the exact words from the author, the paraphrase is too closely related to the original. Again, the source is not cited.

> **Example 3: Culture** can affect **a country's economic performance**. Over time, **a particular culture may produce people with** certain **behavior traits**.

How Can Writers Avoid Plagiarism?

When using information from other sources, the sources must always be acknowledged. By providing an accurate and full description of the sources used, the writer can avoid plagiarism, and the reader can find the original work. This is done in two stages:

1. By providing a parenthetical citation, called an **in-text citation**, within the text. In most scientific fields a numerical reference (e.g., [3]) is noted at the end of the borrowed information. Note that the citation appears in the sentence, not after the period.

> **Example 1**: Data analysis is only one of many challenges presented by Big Data [1].

The reader can find the full details of Reference 1 in the reference list at the end of the work.

2. By providing a **References** page at the end of the work, providing enough information for the reader to find the original source material.

> **Example 2**:
>
> [1]   C. L. P. Chen and C.-Y. Zhang, "Data-intensive applications, challenges, techniques and technologies: A survey on Big Data," *Inf. Sci. (Ny).*, vol. 275, pp. 314–347, Aug. 2014.

On the References page, the reader can find the author, title, and other important details.

What Style Should In-Text Citations and the References Page Follow?

Citation style varies by scientific discipline. Almost all engineers use IEEE style, but the natural sciences use a range of styles. It is best to check expectations with your department, and to use what they recommend. This book is largely written in the IEEE style, and most other scientific styles have similar in-text citations.

2 In-Text Citations

In most scientific disciplines, in-text citations are simply numbers at the end of the piece of information, e.g., [1]. The first citation is numbered 1, the second 2, and so on. If the same source is used later in the same piece of work, it is identified with the same number again. Citation numbers may therefore appear out of order, e.g., 1, 2, 1, 3, 4, 5, 2, 6. Page numbers may be added if the original source is long, e.g., [2, p. 7], but no further information is usually given. Note that p means *page*, and *pp* means *pages* in most styles. Page numbers should only be used if necessary, e.g., in longer texts such as books; it is not common to cite pages for journal articles.

The following table gives an overview of in-text citations for popular styles in scientific writing. Since in-text citations typically occur at the end of a sentence, the period at the end of the sentence is shown here. For example, '.[1]' means that '[1]' appears after the period at the end of the sentence, and '[1].' means that it appears before the period. This table also includes conventions for common specific writing features, e.g., spacing before percentage signs.

Style	In-text citation	et al.†	Numbers	%	SI Units	°	°C
ACS	.[1] or (*1*).	3+	1234 12 345 or 12,345	5%	5 g	5°	5 °C
AMA	.1(pp50–55)	3+	1234 12 345	5%	5 g	5°	5°C
APA	(Kim & Lee, 2020, pp. 50–55).	6+	1,234 12,345	5%	5 g	5°	5 °C
Chicago (=APS)	.[1] or (Kim and Lee 2020, 50–55).	4+	1,234 12,345	5%	5 g	5°	5°C
CSE	.[1] or (Kim and Lee 2020, pp. 50–55)	3+	1234 12 345	5%	5 g	5°	5°C
Harvard‡	(Kim & Lee 2020, pp. 50–55).	4+					
IEEE	[1, pp. 50–55].	3+	1234 12 345	5 %	5 g	5°	5 °C
MLA	(Kim and Lee 50–55).	3+	1,234 12,345	5%	5 g	5°	5°C
Nature	.[1]	6+	1,234 12,345	5%	5 g	5°	5°C
Vancouver‡(=NLM)	.(1 p50–55) or .[1 p50–55] or .[1(p50–55)]	3+					

† Use *et al.* (Latin: *and others*) in in-text citations for sources with n+ authors. For example, in a style that requires et al. for 3+ authors, a paper written by Kim, Lee, Choi, and Park would be cited as "Kim et al." or "Kim, Lee, et al.", but not as "Kim, Lee, Choi, et al." because *al* is plural. The numbers (n) here refer only to in-text citations, not to reference lists.

‡ This is only a citation style, so it does not guide other aspects of writing style.

3 Quotations

Direct quotes are common in many academic fields, but scientific documents rarely use direct quotes [1, p. 512, 2, p. 217]. Nevertheless, scientific writing includes occasional quotes, for example when confirming or disputing other researchers' claims, e.g.:

These results place doubt on Smith's conclusion that "this reaction only occurs when alkali metals are present."

References

[1] H. F. Ebel, C. Bliefert, and W. E. Russey, *The art of scientific writing: From student reports to professional publications in chemistry and related fields*, 2nd ed. Weinheim: Wiley-VCH, 2004.

[2] M. S. Robinson, F. L. Stoller, M. S. Costanza-Robinson, and J. K. Jones, *Write like a chemist: A guide and resource*. Oxford: Oxford University Press, 2008.

Reference Lists

Reference lists differ by citation style, but it is typical for them to appear at the end of a piece of work. Some typical scientific citation styles are exemplified below, each with the same references: a book, and a journal article. IEEE is considered in more detail at the beginning of this list, as students of many disciplines use this style.

Institute of Electrical and Electronics Engineers (IEEE)

Print documents

Journal Article

[1]   C. Bhandari, R. H. W. Hoppe, and R. Kumar, "A C^0 interior penalty discontinuous Galerkin method for fourth-order total variation flow. II: Existence and uniqueness," *Numer. Methods Partial Differ. Equ.*, vol. 35, no. 4, pp. 1477–1496, 2019.

Book by One Author

[2]   J. Stewart, *Calculus: Concepts and Contexts, Enhanced.* Boston, MA: Cengage Learning, 2018.

Book by Three or More Authors

[3]   S.-G. Lee, E.-K. Kim, Y. Ham, A. Kumar, R. Beezer, Q.-P. Vu, L. Simon, and S.-G. Hwang, *Calculus.* Seoul: KyungMoonSa, 2014.

Chapter in an Edited Book

[4]   E. R. Blatchley and J. E. Thompson, "Groundwater contaminants," in *The Handbook of Groundwater Engineering*, 3rd ed., J. H. Cushman and D. M. Tartakovsky, Eds. Boca Raton: CRC Press, 2017, pp. 127–148.

Book by an Institutional or Organizational Author

[5]   IEEE Power Engineering Society. Substation Committee, *IEEE Guide for Safety in AC Substation Grounding.* IEEE, 1986.

Manual

[6]   G. Dixon, *The Washing Machine Manual.* Sparkford: Haynes, 1999.

Technical Report

[7]   Naval Civil Engineering Laboratory, "Technical Report" Civil Engineering Laboratory, Naval Construction Battalion Center, Port Hueneme, CA, 1980.

Electronic documents

E-book

[8]   A. Sharma, M. Kumar, S. Kaur, and A. K. Nagpal, *Evaluation of Environmental Contaminants and Natural Products: A Human Health Perspective.* Bentham Science, 2019. doi: 10.2174/97898114109631190101.

Article in an Online Encyclopedia

[9]   M. I. Voitsekhovskii, "Topology of compact convergence," *Encyclopedia of Mathematics.* http://www.encyclopediaofmath.org/index.php?title=Topology_of_compact_convergence (accessed Jun. 28, 2022).

Online Newspaper Article

[10]   BBC News, "Bombardier wing makers win top engineering award," Jul. 12, 2019. https://www.bbc.com/news/uk-northern-ireland-48955394 (accessed Sep. 18, 2019).

Professional Website

[11]   Korea Meteorological Administration, "Observation Network," 2019. http://www.kma.go.kr/eng/biz/observation_01.jsp (accessed Jun. 28, 2022).

General Website

[12]   H. Wright, "Five Lessons from Women in Engineering," *Medium.* https://medium.com/peopleatsiemens/five-lessons-from-women-in-engineering-5f020b37785a (accessed Jun. 28, 2022).

Personal Website

[13]   M. Green, "A Few Thoughts on Cryptographic Engineering." https://blog.cryptographyengineering.com/ (accessed Jun. 28, 2022).

Email

[14]   A. Smith. "Re: Confidential Memo regarding the Stainless Steel Pin Rotors" Personal email (August 25, 2019).

American Chemical Society (ACS)

1.   Lee, S.-G.; Kim, E.-K.; Ham, Y.; Kumar, A.; Beezer, R.; Vu, Q.-P.; Simon, L.; Hwang, S.-G. Calculus; KyungMoonSa: Seoul, 2014.

2.   Bhandari, C.; Hoppe, R. H. W.; Kumar, R. A C0 Interior Penalty Discontinuous Galerkin Method for Fourth-Order Total Variation Flow. II: Existence and Uniqueness. Numer. Methods Partial Differ. Equ. 2019, 35 (4), 1477–1496. https://doi.org/10.1002/num.22365.

American Medical Association (AMA)

1. Lee S-G, Kim E-K, Ham Y, et al. *Calculus*. Seoul: KyungMoonSa; 2014.
2. Bhandari C, Hoppe RHW, Kumar R. A C^0 interior penalty discontinuous Galerkin method for fourth-order total variation flow. II: Existence and uniqueness. *Numer Methods Partial Differ Equ*. 2019;35(4):1477-1496. doi:10.1002/num.22365.

American Psychological Association (APA)

Bhandari, C., Hoppe, R. H. W., & Kumar, R. (2019). A C0 interior penalty discontinuous Galerkin method for fourth-order total variation flow. II: Existence and uniqueness. *Numerical Methods for Partial Differential Equations, 35*(4), 1477–1496. https://doi.org/10.1002/num.22365

Lee, S.-G., Kim, E.-K., Ham, Y., Kumar, A., Beezer, R., Vu, Q.-P., Simon, L., & Hwang, S.-G. (2014). Calculus. KyungMoonSa.

American Physics Society (APS)

[1]   S.-G. Lee, E.-K. Kim, Y. Ham, A. Kumar, R. Beezer, Q.-P. Vu, L. Simon, and S.-G. Hwang, Calculus (KyungMoonSa, Seoul, 2014).

[2]   C. Bhandari, R. H. W. Hoppe, and R. Kumar, Numer. Methods Partial Differ. Equ. 35, 1477 (2019).

Chicago Manual of Style (=APS)

Bhandari, Chandi, Ronald H.W. Hoppe, and Rahul Kumar. 2019. "A C0 Interior Penalty Discontinuous Galerkin Method for Fourth-Order Total Variation Flow. II: Existence and Uniqueness." *Numerical Methods for Partial Differential Equations* 35 (4): 1477–96. https://doi.org/10.1002/num.22365.

Lee, Sang-Gu, Eung-Ki Kim, Yoonmee Ham, Ajit Kumar, Robert Beezer, Quoc-Phong Vu, Lois Simon, and Suk-Geun Hwang. 2014. *Calculus*. Seoul: KyungMoonSa.

Council of Science Editors (CSE)

1. Bhandari C, Hoppe RHW, Kumar R. A C^0 interior penalty discontinuous Galerkin method for fourth-order total variation flow. II: Existence and uniqueness. Numerical Methods for Partial Differential Equations. 2019 [Accessed 2019 Sep 17];35(4):1477–1496. https://onlinelibrary.wiley.com/doi/abs/10.1002/num.22365. doi:10.1002/num.22365

2. Lee S-G, Kim E-K, Ham Y, Kumar A, Beezer R, Vu Q-P, Simon L, Hwang S-G. Calculus. Seoul: KyungMoonSa; 2014.

Harvard referencing

Bhandari, C., Hoppe, R.H.W., Kumar, R., 2019. A C0 interior penalty discontinuous Galerkin method for fourth-order total variation flow. II: Existence and uniqueness. Numerical Methods for Partial Differential Equations 35, 1477–1496. https://doi.org/10.1002/num.22365

Lee, S.-G., Kim, E.-K., Ham, Y., Kumar, A., Beezer, R., Vu, Q.-P., Simon, L., Hwang, S.-G., 2014. Calculus. KyungMoonSa, Seoul.

Nature

1. Lee, S.-G. *et al. Calculus*. (KyungMoonSa, 2014).

2. Bhandari, C., Hoppe, R. H. W. & Kumar, R. A C^0 interior penalty discontinuous Galerkin method for fourth-order total variation flow. II: Existence and uniqueness. *Numer. Methods Partial Differ. Equ.* 35, 1477–1496 (2019).

Vancouver system

1. Lee SG, Kim EK, Ham Y, Kumar A, Beezer R, Vu QP, et al. Calculus. Seoul: KyungMoonSa; 2014.

2. Bhandari C, Hoppe RHW, Kumar R. A C0 interior penalty discontinuous Galerkin method for fourth-order total variation flow. II: Existence and uniqueness. Numerical Methods for Partial Differential Equations [Internet]. 2019 [cited 2019 Sep 17];35(4):1477–96. Available from: https://onlinelibrary.wiley.com/doi/abs/10.1002/num.22365

5 Reference Management Software

It is very difficult to remember how to cite everything even in one style. For this reason, academics rarely type reference lists manually. Almost all use reference management software. Some of these are free, and many integrate into word processors such as Microsoft Word, and OpenOffice. The most popular of these are Mendeley and Zotero [1], though there are other programs available. It is strongly recommended that students use such a program.

Reference

[1]   Scribendi, "Up close: The 5 best reference management programs." [Online]. Available: https://www.scribendi.com/advice/reference_management_software_solutions.en.html. [Accessed: 17-Sep-2019].

AI and machine translation

Throughout history, plagiarism—the copying of others' work or ideas—has been a problem in society, in law, and in academia. With the advance of artificial intelligence (AI) tools, e.g., ChatGPT, and machine translation (MT), e.g., DeepL, Google Translate, Papago, plagiarism has become more sophisticated, so it is important to discuss appropriate use of this technology.

Throughout history, the development of new technology has met resistance, perhaps especially in education. Indeed, even Socrates claimed that writing would "create forgetfulness in the learners' souls, because they will not use their memories" [1]. It is commonly argued nowadays that use of technology in language education is similar to use of calculators in mathematics lessons. While this analogy may sometimes be appropriate, there can also be differences. A calculator helps with basic arithmetic, so the student can focus on developing more advanced skills. Similarly, a dictionary helps with spelling, leaving the student to focus on writing composition. However, with AI tools such as ChatGPT, almost the entire writing process is skipped, so the student only needs to do the final edit; and with MT tools, the learner's second language writing development may be hindered. It is therefore easy to argue that students' writing may not develop well if they rely on AI or MT tools.

On the other hand, we have these tools, and they will not disappear, so resisting their use can appear counterproductive and futile. AI and MT tools are clearly useful, but they are imperfect, so learners are encouraged to use them with caution, and to practice the writing process themselves, too, so they understand how texts are formed.

It is important in education and business to consider whether AI and MT are forms of plagiarism. In short, the answer is "not necessarily". If we copy others' work into a machine translator, and use the output, then this is clearly plagiarism. If, however, we write in our first language, and use MT to convert that into another language, then that is not necessarily plagiarism. Nevertheless, in an academic context, this is a form of cheating and dishonesty, as it does not demonstrate ability to write in that language. Some universities, e.g., Boğaziçi University [2], University of Cape Town [3], classify this as plagiarism. Whether it is technically plagiarism or not, such use of MT is typically considered unethical academic practice in a second language learning context, and Mundt and Groves argue that this needs "official institutional censure" [4].

Institutions may be tempted to ban AI and MT entirely, but this appears unhelpful and unrealistic: many people carry a smartphone with them everywhere they go, so they constantly have instant access to these tools. Therefore, while embracing technological progress, we must learn when use of AI and MT is appropriate, and when it is not. As these tools continue to improve, they begin to appear more natural. However, they may struggle in several ways. First, they may struggle to identify language genre well. Style differs greatly for example between writing a text message to a friend, writing an apology to a boss, writing a recipe, and writing an experiment report, and Ai and MT are not yet natural in many such genres, so they often create unnatural output. Furthermore, they can struggle with pragmatic meaning, which often depends on context and tone. For example, "That's nice." can mean "That isn't nice.", and "right" can take a range of meanings, e.g., "I understand", "I don't understand", and "I'm leaving," MT also appears not to consider meaning beyond the sentence level., focusing instead on grammar within isolated sentences, while AI-generated text-level flow can be awkward, too. Mundt and Groves also note that MT struggles to adapt text to the social norms of related cultures associated with the target language [4]. There are thus clearly many drawbacks of AI and MT. Of course, they will likely improve, but users must beware that the output is often inappropriate. It is also concerning that reading such output (which can be unnatural or inappropriate) can influence users' future writing [5]. Learners are therefore advised to use AI or MT as they would a dictionary or a calculator: first, they should trust themselves to write their own material; then they can use AI and MT for specific needs, e.g., finding a word, reducing the length of a sentence, or expressing a short phrase; and finally to review and revise the output, adjusting it to integrate it into the text.

Finally, some learners may still wish to use AI and MT to translate or write long text—perhaps even entire reports—to save time, and to cheat on an assignment, perhaps thinking that these tools are undetectable. It is true that extrinsic analysis through tools such as Turnitin™ struggles to identify such output, and detection tools are playing a game of cat and mouse with AI and MT software; however, intrinsic analysis of style can determine whether text was written by one author or several, by a student, or by AI. Experienced teachers are skilled at identifying such text, so students must be warned that excessive AI and MT use will be detected and penalized.

References

[1]   Plato, "Phaedrus," Plat. Phaedrus 275, http://www. http://www.perseus.tufts.edu/hopper/text?doc=urn:cts:greekLit:tlg0059.tlg012.perseus-eng1:275 (accessed Jul. 24, 2023).

[2]   Boğaziçi University Department of Translation and Interpreting Studies, "Academic ethics: Plagiarism." https://transint.boun.edu.tr/academic-ethics-plagiarism (accessed Jul. 12, 2023).

[3] University of Cape Town, "Avoiding plagiarism: A guide for students." Accessed: Jul. 12, 2023. [Online]. Available: https://uct.ac.za/sites/default/files/content_migration/uct_ac_za/39/files/Guide_StudentGuideOnAvoidingPlagiarism.pdf

[4] K. Mundt and M. Groves, "A double-edged sword: The merits and the policy implications of Google Translate in higher education," *European Journal of Higher Education*, vol. 6, no. 4, pp. 387–401, Oct. 2016, doi: 10.1080/21568235.2016.1172248.

[5] N. Resende and A. Way, "Can Google Translate rewire Your L2 English processing?," *Digital*, vol. 1, no. 1, pp. 66–85, Mar. 2021, doi: 10.3390/digital1010006.

After learning about what plagiarism is and how to avoid it, fill out both contracts. Remove the bottom contract, and give it to your professor. Keep the top contract for yourself to remind you about your commitment to academic integrity.

Academic Integrity Contract

I, _____, hereby promise to uphold my credibility by avoiding plagiarism and excessive machine translation in my work. I will cite all the sources that I use from the Internet and elsewhere for all ideas that are not my own. If I am caught plagiarizing, using other people's materials without citation, quoting without citation or without showing that the words are not mine, or using machine translation for lengthy text, then I will accept the consequence of receiving no points for the work.

Date: _____

Name: _____

Student Number: _____ Class: _____

Signature: _____

_____

....

Academic Integrity Contract

I, _____, hereby promise to uphold my credibility by avoiding plagiarism and excessive machine translation in my work. I will cite all the sources that I use from the Internet and elsewhere for all ideas that are not my own. If I am caught plagiarizing, using other people's materials without citation, quoting without citation or without showing that the words are not mine, or using machine translation for lengthy text, then I will accept the consequence of receiving no points for the work.

Date: _____

Name: _____

Student Number: _____ Class: _____

Signature: _____

_____

Absolutely Write
(Revised Edition)

A foundation in academic writing for natural scientists and engineers

Publisher | Ji-Beom Yoo
Printed by | Sungkyunkwan University Press
Publication date | February 16 2024

Writers | Bridget McGregor
          Cameron Bramall
          David Roberts
          Darren Hogan
          Justin Barrass
          Kim Charles Barnett
Project Coordinator | Yoon, Yousook

Sungkyunkwan University Press
25-2 Sungkyunkwan-ro, Jongno-gu
Seoul 03063, Korea
Tel: 82-2-760-1253~4, Fax: 82-2-762-7452
http://press.skku.edu

ISBN 979-11-5550-624-0 13740